Reintroducing Nature into Health and Wellbeing

Janaka Jayawickrama · Devendraraj Madhanagopal

Reintroducing Nature into Health and Wellbeing

Learnings from Ancient South Asia

Janaka Jayawickrama ⓘ
Department of History
Research Centre for Health and Wellbeing
College of Liberal Arts
Shanghai University
Shanghai, China

Devendraraj Madhanagopal ⓘ
School of Sustainability
XIM University
Bhubaneswar, Odisha, India

ISBN 978-981-96-3089-9   ISBN 978-981-96-3090-5 (eBook)
https://doi.org/10.1007/978-981-96-3090-5

© The Editor(s) (if applicable) and The Author(s), under exclusive license to Springer Nature Singapore Pte Ltd. 2025

This work is subject to copyright. All rights are solely and exclusively licensed by the Publisher, whether the whole or part of the material is concerned, specifically the rights of translation, reprinting, reuse of illustrations, recitation, broadcasting, reproduction on microfilms or in any other physical way, and transmission or information storage and retrieval, electronic adaptation, computer software, or by similar or dissimilar methodology now known or hereafter developed.
The use of general descriptive names, registered names, trademarks, service marks, etc. in this publication does not imply, even in the absence of a specific statement, that such names are exempt from the relevant protective laws and regulations and therefore free for general use.
The publisher, the authors and the editors are safe to assume that the advice and information in this book are believed to be true and accurate at the date of publication. Neither the publisher nor the authors or the editors give a warranty, expressed or implied, with respect to the material contained herein or for any errors or omissions that may have been made. The publisher remains neutral with regard to jurisdictional claims in published maps and institutional affiliations.

This Springer imprint is published by the registered company Springer Nature Singapore Pte Ltd.
The registered company address is: 152 Beach Road, #21-01/04 Gateway East, Singapore 189721, Singapore

If disposing of this product, please recycle the paper.

To our parents, who represent the past
To our wives, who represent the present
To our children, who represent the future

Preface

We arrived at the same place through different paths. Growing up in rural Sri Lanka and India respectively, we both observed the health and wellbeing challenges of people through poverty, disasters, and conflicts since 1970s. Our learning experiences started from people themselves. Health, we understood early on as a combination of physical, mental and spiritual experience. Life keeps throwing various challenges—both positive and negative—at individuals, and their ability to deal with them decides their wellbeing. In that, many people helped us to draw our understandings. We want to acknowledge and appreciate all the communities from our native lands and many other parts of the world for teaching us. They have made us humble, compassionate, and, most notably, care about this planet, our home.

We would be remiss if we did not acknowledge the significance of the learnings, we had from Appuhami, Siriwardhane, Madanayake, Nadaraja, Wimala, Rameeza, Thilak, Khadija, Paul, Ken, Nagu, Javita, Jayan, Jenny, Jan, Amanda, Sarah, and many individuals from communities we lived and worked across the world. Thank you as well for the possibility, in some cases, of being part of the struggles, conversations, and reflexive praxis, and, in—others, of being able to dialogue and/or think "with".

This book is an outcome of numerous conversations and debates we had with many mentors, colleagues, and friends. The Rev. Dr. John R. Van Eenwyk, Dr. Alison Eyre, Dr. Ponna Wignaraja, Dr. Derek Summerfield, late Prof. Phil O'Keefe, late Prof. Kriben Pillay, Prof. Karl Atkin, Dr. Anu Pillay, Dr. Ramani Jayasundere, Dr. Claudia Adler, late Dr. Mariam Conteh, late Dr. Geoff O'Brien, Mr. Douglas Chandana Kumara, Dr. Aishwarya Vidyasagaran, Dr. Jerome Wright, Prof. Zhiguang Yin, Dr. Yunqing Xu, Dr. Lei Zhou and many others. They have provided us with space for creative debates and arguments to understand different aspects of health and wellbeing.

We were really lucky to have established our discussions with Prof. Walter Mignolo. He pushed us to think beyond our limitations and continue to point out the pitfalls of coloniality. Professor Mignolo showed us the importance of continued engagement with notions even when we do not agree with them. Our writing shaped us through the experiences of the Global South. We realised that the world looks different from where we are now—China and India. However, we think that the

Global South is not just a geography, but an idea. An idea of dignity, compassion, and care for all. The ideas we present in this book can be understood as an invitation for all the readers to engage with concepts with an open mind.

The world needs more and more discussions, dialogues, and debates on health and wellbeing than ever. The human population continues to prove that they are highly incapable of caring for themselves, each other, and this planet. The climate crisis combined with all the wars, uneven development challenges, and technological hazards are pushing human population for possible extinction. In that, we sincerely thank our universities (Shanghai University, China, and XIM University, Bhubaneswar, India) for all the support that they provided us in working on this book. We would like to thank our colleagues—Prof. Yong'an Zhang, Dr. Arnab Chakraborty, Prof. Yun Xia, and Dr. Yue Gu who has been collaborating with us on health and wellbeing. Their friendship and kindness cannot be forgotten in this book.

Finally, we would like to thank our biggest supporters—Kamani and Priyadarshini. Their love, compassion, and care have nurtured us to be better. The two bundles of joy in our lives—Tikiri and Chittaroopa—have been reminding us why we are doing what we are doing!

Shanghai, China	Janaka Jayawickrama
Bhubaneswar, Odisha, India	Devendraraj Madhanagopal

Competing Interests We declare that there are no financial and/or non-financial interests.

Ethics The personal quotations, anecdotes, and stories that are included in this book are derived from the research of both Janaka Jayawickrama and Devendraraj Madhanagopal. All our research has been approved by various ethics committees in Sri Lanka, India, the UK, and China. All the individual quotations that have come through communities are presented with pseudonyms to protect their identities.

Contents

1 **Need for a Broader Thinking Beyond Mainstream** 1
  1.1 Is Our Today's World Prosperous? 1
  1.2 Why Health and Wellbeing? 5
  1.3 Explaining Environment Within Nature 7
  1.4 Suffering Uncertainty and Danger: Seeing Through Ancient
      Philosophical Traditions 10
      1.4.1 Implications of Uncertainty and Dangers on Health
            and Wellbeing 11
  1.5 Traditional Medical Systems in South Asia: Some Selected
      Insights 12
  1.6 Why This Book? 13
      1.6.1 Our Experiences 14
      1.6.2 What Methodological Approach Does This Book
            Take? 16
      1.6.3 What This Book Is Not? 17
  1.7 Organization of the Flow 18
  References 20

2 **The Problem of Biomedical Definitions of Health and Wellbeing** 25
  2.1 Evolution of Health Concepts in Ancient Greek Philosophy
      and Medicine 25
      2.1.1 Debates on the Body, Soul, and Disease 26
      2.1.2 "Harmony" and "Balance" Through the Ages 27
      2.1.3 Mental Disorders in Ancient European Philosophy 27
      2.1.4 Medieval Views on "Natura": Divine to Rational Shift .. 28
  2.2 Health and Wellbeing in European Understanding: A Colonial
      Critical Overview 29
      2.2.1 Perspectives of Malthus, Ricardo, Marx, and Rousseau .. 30
      2.2.2 European Colonialism and Its Impacts on "Knowledge
            Systems" 31
      2.2.3 Health and Wellbeing in Colonized Lands? 32

	2.3	Understanding Western Biomedicine: Origins, Concepts, and Critiques	33
	2.4	Biomedicine Within the Dominant Epistemology	37
	2.5	Ancient Versus Modern Views on Body and Health	38
		2.5.1 Biomedical Definitions of "Health" and "Wellbeing" Through a Critical Lens	39
		2.5.2 Normalization and Correction: Biomedical Definitions Within the Capital Marketplace	40
	2.6	Discussing Health and Wellbeing Minus "Nature": Is It Feasible?	41
		2.6.1 From Typhus to COVID-19: Tracing Medical Sociology Through the Lens of Politics, Media, and Health Narratives	43
		2.6.2 Media, Politics, and Public Health: Where Are the Links?	45
	References	47
3	**Defining Health and Wellbeing Through Ancient South Asian Philosophies**	51
	3.1	The Health Complexities of South Asia	51
		3.1.1 South Asia and the Three Stages of Epidemiological Transition: A Few Questions	52
	3.2	Traditional South Asian Medical Systems	53
	3.3	Defining Health and Wellbeing from Ancient Wisdoms: Ayurveda and Siddha	57
	3.4	Critiques Within: The Case of India	66
	3.5	Taking a Different Epistemology	70
	References	72
4	**Practical Implications and Possible Adaptations**	75
	4.1	Introduction	75
	4.2	Dying from Illness Versus Dying with Illness	76
	4.3	Ancient Understanding(s) and Modern Tensions	80
	4.4	Transformation—A Possibility?	86
	4.5	Implications for Transformation	89
	4.6	Disobeying Euro-North American Epistemology	92
	References	93
5	**Personal and Professional Encounters of Health and Wellbeing: Beyond Medical Sphere**	97
	5.1	Introduction	97
	5.2	Personal Experiences of Health and Wellbeing	97
		5.2.1 Disasters and Crises: Health and Wellbeing	100
	5.3	Encounters with Ayurveda: Insights from India's Southern Region	102
	5.4	Towards a Conclusion	105
	References	108

6	**Towards a New Paradigm**		111
	6.1 Towards a New Paradigm?		111
		6.1.1 Addressing the Challenges of Coloniality and "Epistemology"	112
	6.2 Health and Wellbeing Beyond the Capital Marketplace		115
	6.3 Towards a New Paradigm for Health and Wellbeing		119
	References		123

Index 125

About the Authors

Janaka Jayawickrama is a professor of Social Anthropology in the Department of History and Director—Research Centre for Health and Wellbeing of the College of Liberal Arts, Shanghai University, China. He has researched and published widely on issues of health and wellbeing, especially related to disasters, conflicts, and uneven development. His work has been influential in global policies on humanitarian responses and bringing the voices of communities into policies.

Devendraraj Madhanagopal is an assistant professor at the School of Sustainability, XIM University, Odisha, India. He has conducted research on various topics, including environmental sociology, environmental governance, social and political dimensions of climate change, environmental justice, climate justice, and social inclusion. He is the author of a book monograph with Routledge and the lead editor of three edited volumes with Springer Nature and Routledge.

Abbreviations

COVID-19	Corona Virus Disease 2019
CRED	Centre for Research on the Epidemiology of Disasters
DDT	Dichlorodiphenyltrichloroethane
DNA	Deoxyribonucleic Acid
DMIP	Disaster Management and Information Programme
ENT	Ear, Nose, and Throat
GP	General Practitioner
HIC	High-Income Countries
HIV/AIDS	Human Immunodeficiency Virus/Acquired Immunodeficiency Syndrome
IFI	International Financial Institutions
LMIC	Low-and-Middle Income Countries
MIC	Middle-Income Countries
NCD	Non-Communicable Diseases
SSRI	Selective Serotonin Reuptake Inhibitor
TB	Tuberculosis
UK	United Kingdom
UNDP	United Nations Development Programme
UNESCO	United Nations Educational, Cultural, and Scientific Organization
USA	United States of America
WHO	World Health Organization

Chapter 1
Need for a Broader Thinking Beyond Mainstream

"The other day I received a solicitation from a medical foundation, and was surprised by the first sentence, which said: "Imagine a world free of disease." That's inhuman! There can't be a world free of disease. Disease is part of what life is about."

Arthur Kleinman

Q & A with Arthur Kleinman, in Boston Globe (quoted in Blume, 2006)

1.1 Is Our Today's World Prosperous?

More than half of human populations in today's world have access to adequate food and better healthcare systems, resulting in decent longevity and fast transportation and telecommunication facilities—unprecedented over the last thousands of years. This has all become possible due to scientific and technological advancements over the past few decades. Primarily due to breakthroughs in medical sciences[1] over the past few decades, including the development of several vaccinations and therapeutic interventions, humans have continued to increase their longevity and as well as prosperity. At the outset of this book, we strongly acknowledge that we have achieved greater material comforts than previous generations. Household machinery, automobiles, and mobile technologies have enhanced our freedom, transportation, and telecommunication facilities, increasing our ability to connect with people worldwide. Recent estimates state that more than four billion people today have experienced greater prosperity and wellbeing than in past generations.

Nevertheless, we also have a contrasting picture of this encouraging narrative. According to the Global Multidimensional Poverty Index (UNDP-OPHI, 2023), there are 1.1 billion people who are suffering from poverty in 110 countries worldwide.

---

[1] Medical sciences can be understood as the practice of caring for patients, managing the diagnosis, prediction, prevention, treatment, mitigation of their injury or disease, and promoting their health (Firth, 2020; Saunders, 2000).

© The Author(s), under exclusive license to Springer Nature Singapore Pte Ltd. 2025
J. Jayawickrama and D. Madhanagopal, *Reintroducing Nature into Health and Wellbeing*, https://doi.org/10.1007/978-981-96-3090-5_1

Half of all poor people are living in Sub-Saharan Africa, while over a third of all poor people live in South Asia. Nearly two-thirds of all poor people live in middle-income countries (MICs). Of the 1.1 billion people living in poverty, 566 million are children under 18, and 84% reside in rural areas. Rural areas are poorer than urban areas in almost every region of the world. From a health perspective, 824–991 million out of the 1.1 billion poor people do not have access to decent sanitation, housing, or cooking fuel facilities. Further, around 600 million poor people live with at least one person who is undernourished in their household. In South Asia and Sub-Saharan Africa, around 245 million poor people suffer from malnutrition (UNDP, 2023). According to the World Bank, poor people face disproportionate challenges in getting access to decent and adequate health, education, housing, water and sanitation, and hygiene facilities, affecting their wellbeing (World Bank, 2022).

Inequalities due to poverty and uneven development continue to affect the health and wellbeing of billions of human beings across the poor nations worldwide. As per the World Health Organization (WHO), the burden of diseases—both infectious and non-communicable—shows a distinct difference between high- and low-income countries. In 2019, 87.8% of deaths in high-income countries (HIC) were due to non-communicable diseases (NCDs). In the same year, the low-and-middle-income countries (LMIC) experienced a greater burden of infectious diseases, including TB, HIV, malaria, neglected communicable diseases, and hepatitis B (WHO, 2022). Malnutrition across different age groups, addictions, and mental health disorders are affecting individuals regardless of their socioeconomic status. The rise of epidemic and pandemic threats, as well as environmental risks, environment, and climate change, pose additional risks to the health and wellbeing of billions. Furthermore, it has become increasingly evident over the past five decades that human beings can inflict violence and destruction upon themselves, their communities, and the environment (Cissé et al., 2022; Levy & Patz, 2015).

Wars, religious, and ethnic conflicts continue to deprive millions of families of losing their native lands and material belongings and render them refugees and displaced in many regions of the world; floods, cyclones, and earthquakes continue to potentially destroy millions of people's livelihoods and push them into dire poverty and hopelessness. This is particularly high in South Asian nations such as Afghanistan, India, Bangladesh, Sri Lanka, and Pakistan. Adding to this, rising inflation and the loss of middle-level and blue-collar employment opportunities due to growing technology are hitting even rich countries. These are stark reminders of the precariousness of everyday lives that can potentially disrupt human health and wellbeing in multiple ways. Furthermore, illnesses, road accidents, and industrial and technological hazards serve as persistent reminders of the inherent dangers of existence. Notwithstanding the efforts of security professionals, insurance agents, and risk reduction specialists to promote the possibility of external forces obstructing such obstacles, the forces mentioned above highlight the unpredictable and risky nature of human lives, regardless of geographical locations or other factors. Importantly, most of these uncertainties and risks lie outside the ambit of human control.

1.1 Is Our Today's World Prosperous?

Today's world is dominated by the capital marketplace, which continues to be promoted through the extension of colonial projects and globalization. Since independence from the British Empire in South Asia, the development discourse has been caught up in false discourse. The tensions between socialism and capitalism and between tradition and modernism. The elites of many South Asian nations took hold of the governance and pushed people for modernity, which originated from Europe and North America. Mainly because they were educated in Europe and North America. In most cases, they did not have roots within the social and cultural aspects of South Asia, which led to capitalism becoming a dominant paradigm for development in South Asia. However, as argued by the Peruvian sociologist Aníbal Quijano, we explain the challenges of Western modernity within health and wellbeing through the concept of coloniality (Quijano, 2000, 2007). Coloniality indirectly imposes a sense of inadequacy on us for not being what modernity dictates us to do. For instance, the inability to speak English in a "standardized" way is often considered a barrier to finding and getting into better jobs and other livelihood opportunities. Another typical example is the way in which the traditional physicians of South Asia are being treated in medical fields. They are often seen as unfit to treat many ailments and diseases as many do not speak English fluently, and they can function only in their native languages. This is a simple yet complex example of coloniality in the discourse of health and wellbeing.

Contemporary mainstream knowledge results in compartmentalization, a division of knowledge due to Adam Smith's division of labour (Smith, 1776). For example, this compartmentalized learning, and treatments govern institutional education and health systems (Illich, 1973). Education is delivered in a classroom by a trained professional, and health has become specified and is delivered only by a specialist (Illich, 1971). While there is a usefulness in the specialism, this also creates a disconnection. This notion of division or compartmentalization is promoted within societies as an achievement or self-made (Ngomane, 2019). This idea of achievement, whether economic or personal gain, is so dominant within societies that the individual becomes self-centred and completely overlooks the connection to nature and natural processes.

Although written in the context of Maori as an anthropologist, Linda Tuhiwai Smith (1999, p. 25) explains the difference between the Global North and Global South from an epistemological perspective:

> One of the supposed characteristics of primitive peoples was that we could not use our minds or intellects. We could not invent things, we could not create institutions or history, we could not imagine, we could not produce anything of value, we did not know how to use land and other resources from the natural world, we did not practice the 'arts' of civilization. By lacking such values, we disqualified ourselves, not just from civilization but from humanity itself. In other words, we were not 'fully human'; some of us were not even considered partially human. Ideas about what counted as human in association with the power to define people as human or not human were already encoded in imperial and colonial discourses prior to the period of imperialism covered here.

One could argue that Linda Smith's point is a one-off comment about a Maori woman who became an anthropologist. However, the forefathers of the European

Enlightenment clearly understood the concept of "universal humanity." Immanuel Kant in 1764 posited that Africans inherently lacked emotions, stating that African natives naturally do not have significant feelings (Frierson & Guyer, 2012). Further, Georg Wilhelm Friedrich Hegel (1770–1831) echoed similar sentiments, asserting that non-European "races" were inferior, lacking value, and devoid of progress potential (Andrews, 2022). The following statement by Thomas Babington Macaulay—the British politician and historian, dated the 2nd of February 1835—explains the superiority of European (and North American today) knowledge to any other civilization:

> I have never found one among them who could deny that a single shelf of a good European library was worth the whole native literature of India and Arabia.... neither as the languages of law nor as the languages of religion have the Sanscrit and Arabic any peculiar claim to our encouragement. We must at present do our best to form a class who may be interpreters between us and the millions whom we govern, —a class of persons Indian in blood and colour, but English in tastes, in opinions, in morals and in intellect. (Macaulay, 1835)

While humans are responsible for much of the chaos happening on this planet, not all humans but a subset living in the space of Global North are primarily responsible for this crisis (Angus, 2016; Salminen & Vadén, 2015; Valtonen et al., 2020). The failure of this division, especially from a knowledge point of view, has been documented by many scholars (Fanon, 2005; Illich, 1973; Jayawickrama, 2023; Rodney, 1972; Smith & O'Keefe, 1980; Zelinsky, 1975). Also, it has become clear that colonialism and capitalism have been all about theft. Now, those stealing outside their countries are stealing from their own people. As the gap of uneven development widens in Europe and North America, people have been shocked by their experiences that colonialism and capitalism treat them in the same way in which they have treated all the other people of the world. If suffering, from individual to society, through violence, destruction, and discrimination, continues to escalate, the survival of the human species may be at stake. Imagine if there are no humans on this planet. We can well envisage that the planet will flourish.

We summarize our insights on coloniality, modernity, and decoloniality as follows, referring to these scholarly works: Quijano and Wallerstein (1992), Quijano (2000, 2007), Mignolo (2002, 2011, 2021):

1. Modernity is a continuation of coloniality.
2. Coloniality is strongly linked to epistemology.
3. Decoloniality can only happen through decolonization of the mind.

Modern technology, rooted in Western modernity, continues to generate prosperity as well as unpredictable risks. Under globalized capitalism, humans assume they produce nature (Smith & O'Keefe, 1980). Science and technology, including mainstream biomedicine, have been functioning within the globalized capitalism.[2] In that, we have changed our relationship with nature from harmony and compliance to one attempting to dominate, even if this is never fully achieved. We argue that,

---

[2] We use the term biomedicine with terms such as western biomedical approaches, and mainstream biomedicine to refer to the biomedicine that has been dominating health services in South Asia.

in modernity, we have changed our relationship with each other as individuals and communities. Most interestingly, these changes have changed the nature of the risks we face in our modern society.

These risks can be understood through various examples. Land-use change increases the risks of floods, earthquake risks are increased through fracking, and building structures in the mountains increase landslide risks. It is not only the physical aspects of nature but the biological aspects of risks—for example, human immunodeficiency virus/acquired immunodeficiency syndrome (HIV/AIDS), epidemics such as Ebola and COVID-19 outbreaks. Modern science and technology, including nuclear engineering and biotechnologies, continue to produce risks.

Due to their duality of engaging with nature, within coloniality/modernity, science and technology generate only limited solutions to the problems. On the one hand, the human population is part of nature; on the other hand, nature is "external" to humans. However, capitalism, an essential ingredient of Western modernity, attempts to produce nature for values, markets, and exchange. We argue that new risks are produced by modernity and that science and technology cannot control or manage them.

Hence, though today's world has seen socioeconomic and political prosperity compared to previous decades, it continues to grapple with unprecedented global and regional challenges—these challenges come from multiple fronts, such as the environment, politics, and society. Interestingly, several of these challenges are rooted in the technological advances that humankind has continued to accumulate over the past century. To address the massive challenges of newly produced dangers and risks to humans, non-humans, and the natural world and its resulting impact on health and wellbeing, we need to adopt a holistic, collaborative, and mutual learning approach that considers the interconnectedness of risks, their impacts on individuals and communities, and the potential for adaptive solutions that emerge from ancient philosophies and traditional medical systems. Given the factors, it is necessary to revisit and re-evaluate the prevalent and widely accepted and dominated lens of health and wellbeing from a fresh perspective, which is the central focus of this book.

1.2 Why Health and Wellbeing?

In 1948, the WHO defined health as *"a state of complete physical, mental, and social wellbeing and not merely the absence of disease or infirmity."* This definition implies that health is more than the absence of disorders or disabilities. The WHO emphasizes that true wellbeing includes realizing one's full potential, managing normal stressors, maintaining productivity, and contributing positively to one's community. Nevertheless, the contemporary dynamic sociopolitical, cultural, economic, and environmental factors globally and locally have rendered the WHO definition of health and wellbeing unrealistic and inappropriate (Jadad & O'Grady, 2008; Larson, 1999; Smith, 2008).

In recent decades, climate change and growing environmental risks have increasingly threatened the health and wellbeing of all living beings, including humans worldwide. Natural hazards such as floods, droughts, earthquakes, and landslides increase health risks, especially for impoverished people. Climate change and variability, including extreme temperatures, air pollution, and disasters, are some of the major threats to health and wellbeing (Haines et al., 2014). Environmental hazards, such as air and water pollution and hazardous material exposure, can seriously affect human health, causing respiratory and cardiovascular disease, cancer, and brain damage (WHO, 2021). Importantly, climate change has become one of the major and formidable threats to mental health and psychological wellbeing for marginalized and vulnerable sections of our society, including indigenous communities, elderly people, and climate migrants (Hayes et al., 2018; Ramadan & Ataallah, 2021; White et al., 2023). Changes in precipitation patterns can lead to water scarcity and increased risk of waterborne diseases (WHO, 2021). We have yet to understand how pathogens change their reproductive patterns and behaviours. Research also highlights that climate change has multiple indirect impacts on mental health, including increased stress, anxiety, and depression due to displacement and loss of livelihoods (Berry et al., 2018).

Marginalized sections of society—children, the elderly, and people with pre-existing health conditions—are particularly vulnerable to climate change. Starvation, and infectious disease epidemics are just a few examples of how geopolitical threats, such as war, forced displacement, and extreme violence, can negatively affect people's health and wellbeing (Spiegel et al., 2010). Furthermore, nuclear threats, including nuclear accidents and wars, could have disastrous effects on both human health and nature. Considering these risks, health and wellbeing must be understood as the capacity of individuals and communities to manage their increasingly complex interactions with nature effectively. This includes not only the prevention and treatment of illness but also the promotion of resilience and adaptation to these risks (McMichael, 1993).

We assert that the major shortcoming of the WHO definition of health and wellbeing is its inclusion of the term "complete," which has led to the "medicalization of society." According to Kleinman (2006), as presented at the beginning of this Chapter, complete freedom from diseases is inhuman. Smith (2008) argued that this requirement for complete health would make most of us fall into the category of "unhealthy" in most cases. In return, this definition supports the pharmaceutical and biomedical industries, in connection with professional associations, in redefining health and wellbeing and expanding their markets for business. Interestingly, the WHO definition has not been re-evaluated or revised since 1948 despite the dramatic transformation of societal health and wellbeing challenges over the last several decades. Humans have increased the ways they instigate violence against each other, not just in wars and conflicts but also through violence against women, child abuse, and workplace harassment. Additionally, structural and institutional violence, such as professional misconduct and negligence in controlling environmental pollution and following the safety guidelines of hazardous industries, contribute to the adverse health and wellbeing of people. Despite multiple challenges, the WHO definition has not considered or adapted to the varying shifts to health and wellbeing that come from science, technology, environment, climate, and geopolitical risks; therefore, we assert that this definition may even be counterproductive.

Historically, in Asian cultures, there were built-in methods of consensus-making.[3] One example is the republican tradition of the Licchavis in ancient South Asia, renowned for their republican government (Encyclopaedia Britannica, 2010). In describing Ram Rajya (a good society) in Ramayanam, the great Tamil poet Kambar (1180 CE–1250 CE) says that everyone had enough, and no one had more than enough (Nandakumar, 1971). Confucius argued that people need a good environment with good representations and a good economy before thinking and acting appropriately (Rainey, 2010). Buddhist and Hindu philosophical systems represent important ancient philosophies of Asia.[4] To examine the complexities of the present, we emphasize of revisiting into the past, and what ancient philosophical systems of Asia, particularly those of the Indian subcontinent discussed about nature and morality.[5] Discussions on health and wellbeing necessitate a larger perspective and it cannot be confined only with colonialism, markets, and corporates. To advance these discussions, we also need to focus on nature, environment, environmental ethics, anthropocentrism, and morality which we will address in the forthcoming portions.

1.3 Explaining Environment Within Nature

The history of this planet and humankind has been shaped by nature, the environment, and the climate (Frankopan, 2023).[6] Frankopan (2023) argues that humans have re-designed the resources of this planet for positive and negative purposes. For Zoroastrians, the oldest organized faiths that emerged from ancient Persia (contemporary Iran), nature was regarded as a source of joy, which required protection against the destructive habits of human behaviour (Nigosian, 1993). The focus on goodness and purity meant, for example, that Persian societies understood the importance of not polluting water sources and introduced safeguards to ensure this did not occur (Foltz & Saadi-nejad, 2008). Deforestation and notion against tree-cutting

---

[3] Ancient cultural and philosophical knowledge systems in Asia are interconnected and linked through a shared understanding of life, living, and nature. We use the terms Asia and South Asia in this book interchangeably according to the context.

[4] Although both Hindu and Buddhist philosophies originated from the Indian subcontinent, they have impacted Asia as a whole, especially regarding health and wellbeing. These include, but are not limited to, Traditional Chinese Medicine and Traditional Thai Medicine.

[5] We use the term Indian subcontinent here because, before the arrival of the European colonizers, there were no specific countries in this region. However, Nepal was a Kingdom, and Sri Lanka was a separate entity as an island. The Indian subcontinent consists of present-day India, Nepal, Bhutan, Bangladesh, Sri Lanka, Pakistan, and Afghanistan and is called South Asia.

[6] We argue that the terms nature and environment are not synonyms. Nature governs this planet through natural processes, of which human beings are part. The environment is what humans create, including the built environment.

were concerns in Asia even thousands of years ago. This reflects the thoughts of ancient societies in Asia in maintaining benign natural conditions to ensure plentiful harvests and adequate water supply. In 524 BCE, Duke Mu of Shan (an official at the court of Zhou King) warned of the dangers of cutting down forests; otherwise, "the forces of the people will be weakened" (Frankopan, 2023, p. 155). In 243 BCE, the court of Ashoka associated drought with cutting down trees with drought and issued an edict to forbid damaging forests (Thapar, 2012). This was part of a strategy aimed at protecting wildlife and the environment so as to maintain a balance between human development and nature, including a commitment to preventing over-exploitation, which was regarded as unsustainable and inconsistent with responsible government. Respect for the environment became identified with enlightened leadership and good governance. The Arthasastra by Kautilya (third century BCE) advocated protection of the environment for the good of the State. Similarly, Oikonomikos by Xenophon (fourth century BCE) says: "The earth willingly treats righteousness to those who can learn. For the better she is treated, the better things she gives in return" (Cited in Frankopan, 2023, p. 157). Exploitation damaged the earth and reflected a more fundamental moral failing on the part of humankind (Starr, 2012).

Ancient literature from Asia possesses substantial instances of people's participation and self-governing practice at the base of the system alongside wise and compassionate leadership at the top. Democratic consensus-making used to be a part of the tribal mode of governance in ancient Asia (Wignaraja, 1991). Peer pressure was a major deterrent to corrupt practices, establishing societal checks and balances. It also extended to everyday activities such as taking loans and credits, where peer pressure ensures repayment. An open information system at the community level further reinforced the principle of equity, checks and balances, and accountability. Democracy in labour relations, exchange labour, joint ownership of land, and other productive assets further reinforced cooperative values, mutual aid, and equity. The most critical aspect is that the realization of all-inclusivity paved the way for people to live in harmony with natural processes and the environment. While these philosophies and political processes deserve further discussion and evaluation, they are presented succinctly here as general examples.

The environment became a critical dimension of the global discussion on development when the report of the World Commission on Environment and Development, Our Common Future, was published (World Commission on Environment & Development, 1987). Since then, "environment" has been inextricably linked with much research, policy, and practice areas. Ecology, environment systems, environmental health, and environmental justice are some terms we hear in development discourse. As noted by Sachs (2010), scientists and experts often use the terms environment and nature interchangeably in many instances. This has contributed to the widening gap between humans and nature, resulting in corresponding divergence in our understanding of health and wellbeing. On the one side, we expect nature to provide clean air and drinking water.

Conversely, we attempt to control and exploit nature in all possible ways. This contradiction has created more confusion, especially in the discourse of health and wellbeing. Instead of submitting ourselves as a part of nature, humans have increasingly started perceiving themselves as the creators of the environment. Many universities worldwide (in Europe and North America) teach "built environment," which we opine that resulted from this confusion. In contrast, several traditional and Indigenous communities have continued to maintain close ties with nature for generations and centuries; even today, they act as the custodians of natural resources, and they are experts in extracting resources with respect and without harming all living and non-living beings in the forest. Despite lacking formal education, these communities offer insights into sustainability through their intergenerational knowledge and traditional wisdom, often surpassing the understanding of sustainability scientists or experts.

Many rural communities in economically challenged countries in Asia, Africa, Latin/South America, and the Middle East (or West Asia, where we are positioned) do not need to wait for specialists from hastily founded research institutes on sustainable agriculture to deliver solutions to environmental issues such as soil erosion. Provision for future generations has been part of their tribal and peasant practices since immemorial. Moreover, the new centrally or so-called decentralized designed schemes for the "management of environmental resources" threaten to collide with their locally based knowledge about conservation. Their idea of nature is different from the idea of the environment put forward by scientists and experts. This also has multiple negative ramifications for their autonomy and prosperous health and wellbeing in the long term.

Provided all these backgrounds, we attempt to conceptualize our environment as created, influenced, and, in many cases, exploited by human populations. For instance, green spaces and parks in urban settings, alongside buildings, roads, and other infrastructure, are part of the environment. Industrial agriculture and managed natural reserves also fall within this concept. However, we argue that the environment extends beyond human influence. Ancient wisdom and philosophies, not just from South Asia but also from many Indigenous communities, understand that humans, as one of the species of the planet, are governed by nature and natural processes.[7] As argued by Sachs (2010), when nature becomes the object of politics and planning, it becomes the environment. Therefore, throughout this book, we refer to nature and natural processes differently from the environment. Smith and O'Keefe (1980) pointed out that the human attempt to produce nature is one of the failures of the capital marketplace and a method of increasing risks, including health and wellbeing.

European and North American philosophies of utilitarian environmental ethics focus on the long-term wellbeing of humans and ecosystems (Brennan & Lo, 2010). Utilitarianism, in its most traditional form, is both a theory of the good and a theory of the right. It holds that the greatest good is happiness and freedom from pain and suffering, not just for human beings but also beyond. As Brennan and Lo (2010)

---

[7] When it comes to ancient philosophies beyond Europe, many societies in Asia, Africa, Americas (especially Mayans and native Americans), aboriginal, and West Asia share a common thread of their understanding of nature as beyond human capabilities.

explain, these anthropogenic positions critique human-caused environmental degradation if it affects human health and wellbeing. Ultimately, humans and their wellbeing play a prominent role in Western anthropocentrism. To put it simply, Jeremy Bentham's form of utilitarianism advocates that humans should act to maximize happiness or pleasure and minimize suffering or pain, and it poses that the moral value of actions should be judged based on their ability to enhance overall happiness in society (Bentham, 1789, as cited in Bentham, 1970). Nevertheless, the challenge comes through the ideas of division between good and evil and right and wrong. Radhakrishnan (1939) explained that most ancient philosophies, especially those from South Asia, are not about right or wrong and good or bad. We argue that those philosophical thoughts are about the survival of human populations. For example, protecting forests is not a moral or ethical point, but understanding that half of the human breathing apparatus are trees—what we exhale, trees are inhaling, and what trees exhale, we are inhaling. In this realization, the protection of forests becomes a default position.

1.4 Suffering Uncertainty and Danger: Seeing Through Ancient Philosophical Traditions

In many religious and philosophical South Asian traditions such as Hindu, Buddhist, and Jain traditions, suffering through uncertainty and danger is an intrinsic part of human lives. We can also witness such interpretations in Christianity and Islam as well. The Book of Job in the Holy Bible explains that everyone, including righteous people, can, do, and will suffer through the uncertainty and dangers of life. In Islam, the Holy Quran explains that suffering through uncertainty and danger is based on the fundamental notion of the imperfection of human life. According to the Bhagavad Gita, one of the prominent Hindu texts (Radhakrishnan, 1963), humans are frustrated by their attachment to this world and suffer through these conflicting dynamics. Describing these "sufferings" through the uncertainty of life, the Dhammapada, an essential Buddhist text (Radhakrishnan, 1950), notes that all the supports of "being" are unstable. Additionally, it extends its arguments that anything that relies on other things and causes at any time makes everything impermeant. In Jain philosophy, suffering arises from ignorance of the true nature of reality, which is impermanence (Paniker, 2011). In the Sikh philosophical tradition, suffering is associated with human bondage to the impermanence of life. Though suffering is built upon human bondage to impermanence, it is influenced by internal and external factors (Kaur, 1985).

Datta's paper entitled "The moral conception of Nature in Indian philosophy" is one of the oldest and seminal scientific papers on nature in South Asian philosophy. In this, he argues that South Asian theories of nature are fundamentally different from the Western perspectives and explains why. Apart from the Charvaka or allied schools of materialism, of whose systematic account none is available, all South

Asian schools conceive of nature as the stage upon which beings were constituted and guided by righteousness. This applies to both theistic and atheistic traditions—including Buddhism, Jainism, and Mimamsa (Datta, 1936, p. 223). Datta (1936, p. 223–224) clarifies that two components comprise ancient Indian philosophical systems: Organisms and their environments. Organisms refer to the body and the sense organs (indriyas), while the environment consists of everything else outside to them—extra-organic subjects—operates under laws that promote and serve the righteous interests of individuals. The construction of an individual's body and environment in Earth is not arbitrary; it adheres to a law conceived either as the law of a moral world administrator or as an impersonal law that acts spontaneously. This righteous law, broadly known as the conservation of values, equips individuals based on their past actions and strives to ensure and maintain balance. Here, the term "individual" is not limited to humans but includes all sentient beings, from plants to humans and even "Devas,"—superhuman deities. Depending on the school, this law, known by different names like rita, karma, apurva, and adrista, imparts a virtuous dimension to the concept of nature. This goes hand-in-glove with the belief that the very law of truth and righteousness governs both outer and inner worlds.

Notably, the perspectives and visions of the schools of philosophy of ancient South Asia are not monolithic; all the schools differ and as well as overlap in their interpretations of the righteous dimensions of nature, and it has been dialectic. While some Nastika schools, like Buddhism and Jain, seem naturalistic on their surface, all schools, irrespective of their backgrounds, incorporate elements through cosmic laws, unseen principles, or karmic consequences. All the schools reflect a fundamental tie between nature and righteousness in their philosophical perspectives (Datta, 1936). In summary, all different philosophical and spiritual traditions in South Asia have a common thread of understanding that suffering through uncertainty and danger is part of being human or human experience. In terms of elaborating this point within the discourse of health and wellbeing, we further engage with Hindu and Buddhist philosophies as they have a deeper connection with Ayurveda, Siddha, and Deshiya Chikitsa being the most commonly practiced by the majority of the population in the region.

1.4.1 Implications of Uncertainty and Dangers on Health and Wellbeing

In Hindu and Buddhist philosophies, life is perceived as supremely good, offering everyone the opportunity for happiness (Radhakrishnan, 1939). However, there is nothing in this world that is for eternity. Everything, including life, is impermanent and uncertain (Das & Han, 2015; Jayawickrama, 2018; Kleinman, 2006; Radhakrishnan, 1963). As it is well-known, everything around us influence our health and wellbeing—both positively and negatively. This includes plants, trees, insects, sunlight, sounds, buildings, and other physical and chemical systems, and more.

Hence, beyond theoretical understandings, the practicalities of our everyday lives keep reminding us of the uncertain nature of life. In our uncertain and dangerous world, which is surrounded by potential risks, achieving complete health and wellbeing may seem impossible. Nevertheless, it is also not so challenging to develop and implement coherent and inclusive approaches to dealing with uncertainty and risks while ensuring a balance in health and wellbeing. Pandemics such as COVID-19 could hurt the economy and distress millions of families worldwide. In some ways, the COVID-19 epidemic has been beneficial, as it has hastened the transition to renewable energy sources, decreased pollution, and increased funding for conservation initiatives. On the other side, the pandemic has also had negative environmental implications, such as an acceleration of deforestation and an increase in plastic usage, which can have major implications for the environment, health, and wellbeing (Fadare & Okoffo, 2020; Le Quéré et al., 2020; Prata et al., 2020; Tao et al., 2021; Vale et al., 2021).

1.5 Traditional Medical Systems in South Asia: Some Selected Insights

In South Asia, particularly in India and Sri Lanka, the traditional medical systems are deeply rooted in the ancient Hindu and Buddhist philosophical schools, with a few noted exemptions. For example, Ayurveda (knowledge of life), Siddha (perfected one), Naturopathy, Yoga (to unite), and some other paramount traditional medical systems are heavily influenced by Hindu philosophical foundations (Jaiswal & Williams, 2017; Subbarayappa, 1997). In Sri Lanka, the primary traditional medical system, Deshiya Chikitsa (homegrown therapy), is primarily rooted in Buddhist philosophy (De Silva, 2013). Many ancient medical texts, such as Charaka Samhita (second century BCE and the second century CE), Sushruta Samhita (600 BCE–501 BCE), and Sarartha Sangrahaya (398 AD), are classic examples from India and Sri Lanka. Due to the influence and foundations of Hindu and Buddhist philosophies on these medical systems, they share a deeper understanding of illnesses, death, and dying as a natural part of living. These perspectives fundamentally contrast with Euro-North American-centric philosophies that tend to view death and dying as abnormalities. To sum up, roughly, Euro-North American philosophies are founded on the following concepts (Jackson & Riddlesperger, 2003; Jayawickrama, 2010; Kleinman, 2006): (i) Self-discipline, such as Jefferson's concepts of nature and nature is God. (ii) Command of nature by trying to navigate, explore, and colonize the world. (iii) producing and spreading "good" outcomes in societies through activities such as missions to the "Far East" to "save lost souls" and "serve poor people." (iv) denial of human limits, including death, through pushing scientific inventions to find a cure for cancer and cloning. In contrast, Ayurveda recognizes individuals' interconnectedness with their environment and the necessity to align with natural cycles and rhythms to sustain optimal health and wellbeing (Frawley & Ranada, 1994; Patwardhan et al., 2004).

Like this in the forthcoming portions of this book, we discuss other traditional medicinal systems in India and other South Asian countries, including Siddha. In contemporary India, diverse medical options are available, including Western biomedicine, Ayurveda, Homoeopathy, Unani, Siddha, and Gandhian Nature cure, among others. For example, some traditional Siddha physicians of Tamil Nadu, a southern state in India, offer their patients much more than merely curing their physical ailments: the fantasy of a Tamil utopia and even the prospect of immortality (Weiss, 2009, p. 4). Among these traditional medical options, some other options such as "country medicine' (medicines that are produced from organic products and are substantially popular throughout Tamil Nadu), Reiki, tantric practice, goddess worship, and exorcism are also available in South Asia (Weiss, 2009).

1.6 Why This Book?

Provided this background, we, the authors, with some life and academic experiences in social anthropological, sociological, and humanitarian fields, offer insights based on Hindu and Buddhist philosophies. Through this book, we discuss the possibilities of creating an alternative paradigm for understanding the health and wellbeing of humans. We believe that we are in a world where the health and wellbeing sphere is fragmented into physical and mental health—it is further subdivided into various specializations such as ENT, cardiology, nephrology, neurosciences, psychiatry, and clinical psychology (Lerner & Berg, 2015). The evidence reveals that these divisions of health and wellbeing—human and nature, prevention, and treatment— have not culminated in the desired outcome of improved health and wellbeing over the past two centuries. Emphasizing this, this book is one such attempt that draws its foundations and selected insights from Hindu and Buddhist philosophy of oneness, which maintains that our physical and spiritual wellbeing emanates from our connection with nature. The physical environment plays an indispensable role in our health and overall wellbeing. Regrettably, Euro-North American epistemology, the bedrock of biomedical sciences, conceptualizes health and wellbeing, including the WHO's definition of health, perpetuates a schism between the human population and nature.

Emphasizing this in addition to these arguments, we highlight that the notions of "new" thinking and "expertise" need not be exclusively derived from the paradigms of neo- or ultra-modernity. We argue that the "ancient wisdoms" of South Asia can offer insights to relook and confront the risks to health and wellbeing. This book critiques the mainstream definitions, policies, and interventions of health and wellbeing while pointing to a paradigm shift that can enable humans to connect with nature. It argues that this separation deprives humans of the knowledge of their obligation and liability to safeguard their health and wellbeing.

Although we do not aim to criticize WHO's definition of health and wellbeing continuously, throughout this book, we recognize the need to relook health and wellbeing from a different perspective within the context of these criticisms. In the second and third chapters, we explore the historical development of the understanding of health and wellbeing in science and medicine. We examine the relevance and as well as inadequacies of these understandings in dealing with the current and future challenges that humankind faces. In this book, we have chosen to focus on Hindu and Buddhist philosophies from South Asia. This is because Hindu and Buddhist philosophies have distinctively impacted Ayurveda, Siddha, and Deshiya Chikitsa, still practiced by thousands of physicians in contemporary South Asia. Also, both the authors of this book possess selected personal encounters with these medical systems. We bring selected insights from traditional medical approaches advocated in India and Sri Lanka, which are not a new paradigm but rather reiterations of pre-existing ones that were obliterated during the colonial era. As previously stated, this book aims to redefine our understanding of health and wellbeing by drawing from two selected ancient philosophical traditions. Our goal is not only to provide an alternative perspective but also to encourage readers to contemplate our arguments in the background of the authors' own life experiences relevant to the themes of this book. The following section briefly overviews the authors' backgrounds and life experiences. This helps readers understand why we are qualified to present these discussions and deliberations on redefining health and wellbeing for humans.

1.6.1 Our Experiences

Subjected to the European colonial project for 500 years, many current nations of South Asia have endured several tragic violations of their social, cultural, economic, political, and environmental evolution. Over the past 75 years, various social and ethnic divisions and the invasion of the capital marketplace have created several challenges to the health and wellbeing of billions of South Asians. Hence, contemporary South Asia is characterized by stark contradictions between wealth and poverty, health and illness, and education and ignorance, among other disparities. Moreover, over the past five decades, persistent environmental degradation and the hazards of climate change have raised concerns about not just the health and wellbeing of billions of people but also pose threats to the sustainability of humans in the long term. Nevertheless, South Asia boasts a rich cultural and philosophical heritage, including progressive health approaches, sophisticated agricultural mechanisms, innovative pedagogical methods that push philosophical boundaries, and city-states with advanced governing and economic principles. Traditional medical systems that are rooted in Hindu and Buddhist philosophies emphasize the interdependence of persons with their environment, and this is radically different than Western Biomedicine as it not only focuses on curing the patients of disease but also focuses on overall wellbeing, most importantly, balance in life with the nature. Provided this background, we argue that these insights provide solutions to address the complicated challenges of our contemporary world that require multifaceted attention.

1.6 Why This Book?

Both authors have come determined to engage with the subject matter of this book beyond the mainstream research tradition. We argue that a linear scientific analysis is inadequate to examine contemporary challenges to health and wellbeing. The separation of the researcher and the research subject through independence, impartiality, and neutrality is insufficient to generate a meaningful understanding, especially when attempting to bring changes to the subject (Jayawickrama, 2023; Smith & O'Keefe, 1980). In that, our experiences of growing-up in South Asia have a distinct meaning in this book.

The first author of this book spent his formative years in Sri Lanka during the 1970s and 1980s, a time of intense ethnic conflict and the consequent humanitarian crises. He was a witness to the dire poverty endemic to rural Sri Lanka, where preventable diseases like malaria took the toll on several children and farmers resorted to suicide to escape crushing debt burdens; natural hazards such as floods and hurricanes exacerbated the rural distress of millions of peasant communities—decades of civil war in Sri Lanka and the onset of the war in 1983 brought sudden death to the members of his community, which impressed upon him the unpredictability and external risks of life where ordinary people do not have any control. Over this period, he gained vast experience in Sri Lanka as well as international experiences as a humanitarian worker and researcher in different regions of the world, including some of the most disaster and war-hit regions of Africa and West Asia. Through these professional and life experiences, he recognized the limitations of the prevailing approaches to health and wellbeing; he found that these approaches are inadequate to address the multifaceted crises that our societies face. Since 2004, as an academic researcher, he has developed innovative solutions to health and wellbeing, emphasizing constructive contributions over mere criticism.

The book's second author is an academic and researcher from India. He mostly lived and studied in Tamil Nadu and completed his Ph.D. in Mumbai. Over the past five years, he has been based in Odisha, a state in eastern India. He witnessed India's swift economic and technological advancement during his adolescence and twenties, drawing connections to evolving public attitudes regarding health and wellbeing. In the late 2010s, he also observed the abrupt surge in information technology and the sudden bulge of the middle class and how this sudden expansion influenced the overall discourse of health, wellbeing, the environment, and the associated risks. Since 2014, his research has focused on the social and political implications of climate change, environmental conflicts, social movements, and environmental justice-related complications, all of which have significant implications for health and wellbeing. As part of his research activities, he undertook fieldwork in some remote regions of Tamil Nadu, where he witnessed first-hand the social, economic, and health challenges confronting marginalized sectors of society.

Overall, primarily growing-up in South Asia, specifically in Sri Lanka and India during the 1970s to 1990s, both authors experienced diverse health and wellbeing challenges in rural and urban settings. Multiple challenges to infectious diseases such as malaria, TB, and Hepatitis B, natural hazards such as floods, cyclones, hurricanes, and droughts, extreme poverty, conflicts (in the Sri Lankan case), and violence in day-to-day life have increased uncertainties and dangers related to health and wellbeing over the years in South Asia. With this background, in this book, we draw upon selected texts from Hindu and Buddhist philosophies and traditional medical insights of South Asia; we offer critical perspectives that can inform the development of new paradigms for health and wellbeing. While we do not romanticize ancient traditions or dwell in the past, we critically examine these concepts to address the contemporary challenges facing health and wellbeing.

1.6.2 What Methodological Approach Does This Book Take?

The authors of this book have been living and engaging with communities in South Asia since the 1980s, first as members of their respective communities in Sri Lanka and India and then through various collaborations in projects, research, and education in Afghanistan, Bangladesh, Bhutan, India, Maldives, Nepal, Sri Lanka, and Pakistan. In this book, along with scholarly reviews and discussions, the authors attempt to reflect on the insights, anecdotes, and stories they gleaned from their lives and years of working together in the field. Traditional medical systems rooted in Hindu and Buddhist philosophies are the focus of this book, in which the authors draw on personal experience and professional collaboration to analyse a variety of stories and narratives. This is accidental ethnography, and the authors apply it to look back on their lives and the world at large through critical examination and to offer novel insights and perspectives (Levitan et al., 2017). Furthermore, the authors offer scholarly discussions on the connections between environmental problems, climate change, and health and wellbeing challenges. The reflections of these experiences and scholarly discussions are examined through the lens of current health and wellbeing discourse to find a new paradigm.

In this book, we have applied an exploratory literature review method to discuss traditional medical, Hindu, and Buddhist literature. Based on a narrative review framework, this exploratory literature review takes the "traditional" way of reviewing the existing works and is skewed towards a qualitative interpretation of prior knowledge (Sylvester et al., 2013). This exploratory literature review aims to summarize what has been written on research philosophies and approaches with a specific focus on health and wellbeing. However, it does not aim to generalize or cumulate knowledge from what is reviewed (Davies, 2000; Green et al., 2006). This exploratory literature review aims to demonstrate a problem in the current policy and practice of mainstream Western-oriented definitions and operationalization of health and wellbeing. In this regard, the authors have limited their attention to specific literature to make their point. It could be argued that this exploratory review has taken an unsystematic approach, as the selection of literature is subjective, lacks explicit criteria for inclusion, and may lead to prejudiced interpretations (Green et al., 2006). However, it is important to note that many narrative reviews, particularly in the health domain, follow this unstructured approach (Paul et al., 2015; Silva et al., 2015). Our exploratory review approach has the potential to identify gaps in knowledge and generate new knowledge, particularly in rapidly complex and evolving health, wellbeing, and nature.

1.6.3 What This Book Is Not?

This book does not attempt to glorify ancient wisdom, philosophies, and traditions or imply that this can replace modern science and technology. We understand that these traditional medical systems were developed in different social, political, cultural, economic, and environmental contexts in ancient South Asia. Therefore, some approaches and systems may not be relevant to contemporary health and wellbeing challenges. Before the European colonizers arrived, South Asia was not divided into nations as it is today. Instead, this vast land was composed of a collection of numerous kingdoms. Life was not satisfactory and pleasant for everyone as this region experienced numerous wars and disasters, resulting in widespread inequalities in health and wellbeing. Nevertheless, this was also a period where this region buzzed with vital developments in the philosophical traditions and medical systems rooted in different schools of Hindu, Buddhist, and Jain philosophies. Those were also the periods when these knowledge systems were used to fight against inequality and discrimination against certain sections of society. For example, the Buddha (563–483 BCE) used his teachings to resist these oppressions within Hindu approaches. The founder of Jainism, Mahavira, a contemporary to the Buddha, took a similar approach to promote non-violence. In the same way, Adi Shankaracharya (788–820 AD) revived Hindi philosophy and synthesized the Advaita Vedanta teachings during his period.

Despite all these wars, disasters, violence, poverty, and chaos, South Asia had a significant affinity towards seeking wisdom and knowledge. The Nalanda University, founded in 427 BCE in the eastern part of the Indian subcontinent, drew scholars from China, Korea, Japan, Tibet, Mongolia, Sri Lanka, and Southeast Asia for scholarly pursuits. This means ancient South Asia had common spaces for scholars to learn and collaborate, which had a deep-rooted history mutually. In this spirit, this book invites scholars from different backgrounds, traditions, and disciplines to engage with our work critically. We do not propose to bring absolute answers through this book. While acknowledging the significant contributions of science, especially biomedicine, to health and wellbeing, we critically examine the challenges the capital marketplace continues to produce for health and wellbeing. We do not claim that one philosophy, tradition, and approach are supreme and better. On the contrary, we advocate for the readers to learn from all philosophical traditions without prejudiced bias and discrimination to address the contemporary health and wellbeing challenges.

Hence, this is neither a science book nor a book about South Asian traditional medicine or philosophies. We attempt to promote epistemic freedom while critically borrowing certain concepts from all different traditions, including mainstream sciences of the Western world. The Euro-North American epistemology strongly influences contemporary science, education, and research. This goes back to the colonial project and the current capital marketplace, and as Mignolo (2009, 2011) argues, this has created a global epistemic injustice that this book highlights in various instances. One way of knowing has become the dominant approach, and all other ways of knowing are labelled as "primitive" and "unscientific." Unfortunately, we are ignoring the rich tapestry of successful ways of knowing from Asia, Africa, Latin / South America, and the West Asia. Indigenous communities in North America, Australia, and New Zealand had rich and pragmatic ways of knowing (epistemologies), and in most cases, they led comfortable lives. For example, according to Garro (1990), Anishinaabeg people who occupied the territories in the Southeast of Canada and Northeast of the USA did not suffer from major diseases and illnesses before the arrival of European colonizers. Substantial people of these communities used to have longevity that went beyond a hundred years. However, in the contemporary world, their life situations have been spanned with major illnesses and diseases that any other European Canadian or American citizen. As Sinclair (2013) argues, this is mainly because they were oppressed by European epistemology with the introduction of the capital marketplace, where they lost their Indigenous epistemological foundations.

We can learn from different philosophies without discrimination or creating power imbalances through epistemic freedom. It has become evident that the contemporary challenges to health and wellbeing cannot be solved from a single discipline analysis. We invite a collaborative learning process from all different philosophies and traditions to solve contemporary health and wellbeing challenges. We do not argue that we must go back to the history of South Asian philosophical and traditional medical approaches to be exported to other countries without critical thinking. What works in Sri Lanka may not work in Nepal. Likewise, what works in India may not work in the UK or USA. However, there can be a critical analysis of different learning approaches and adapting them according to context.

1.7 Organization of the Flow

This book is intertwined with our autobiographical narratives, community experiences, and contemporary and ancient literature. Following this introduction chapter, Chap. 2: The Problem of Biomedical Definitions of Health and Wellbeing, is based on the critical debates on biomedicine and aims to elaborate on the problems of biomedical definitions and operationalization globally about health and wellbeing. Critiques of the WHO's definition of health and wellbeing as a foundational element will be examined with various other policies, including the Alma Ata Declaration (1978). The key argument of this chapter is to provide evidence of the disjuncture between humans and nature and how this has created more and more health and wellbeing challenges. Humans have become external to nature through scientific methodology while drawing environmental resources. This dichotomous positionality is destroying the health and wellbeing of human populations and the planet on which we live. The biomedical model, while capable of maintaining a long life, is

1.7 Organization of the Flow

insufficient to facilitate the overall health and wellbeing of human populations due to the limitations of scientific analysis.

Chapter 3: Defining Health and Wellbeing through Ancient South Asian Philosophies, takes the influences of Hindu and Buddhist philosophies in India and Sri Lanka in redefining health and wellbeing. Further, an overview of traditional medical systems in Afghanistan, Bangladesh, Bhutan, India, Maldives, Nepal, Sri Lanka, and Pakistan is provided to point out the shared values and principles within philosophical foundations. Traditional medicine and approaches to life in these countries will be explained and examined against the scientific notions of medical interventions. Home to one-fifth of the world's population, South Asia is also a home for people living in dire poverty (World Bank, 2023). South Asia is also infamously known for its low life expectancy and high rates of malnutrition, infant mortality, and the prevalence of TB and HIV/AIDS, only surpassed by sub-Saharan Africa (Hate & Gannon, 2010). The rapid population growth, governance complications, and socioeconomic inequalities in South Asia have already resulted in major health and wellbeing challenges for billions of marginalized populations. These challenges include poor sanitation, poor maternal health, poor access to healthcare services, widespread malaria, and an emerging epidemic of chronic diseases. Moreover, as identified by CRED (2023), natural hazards such as floods, droughts, and landslides have increased in South Asia. The interplay between poverty, disasters, and societal and political conflicts have created major obstacles to the health and wellbeing of humans, which will likely intensify in the future. Importantly, these challenges are not limited to South Asia but extend to the Global South. These challenges intensify the divisions between humans, animals, and nature. Nevertheless, these challenges also provide specific opportunities for humans to employ the traditional medical systems and generational beliefs of South Asians to overcome some of the challenges of health and wellbeing. South Asians' historical engagement with nature and environmental resources can be leveraged to cope with suffering. This chapter provides the readers with learnings from these experiences.

Chapter 4: Practical Implications and Possible Adaptations, identifies the problems, conceptual discussions, and wisdom gleaned from the ancient philosophies of the previous chapter. Chapter four focuses on the rigorous exploration of the practical realities and potential adaptations of health and wellbeing to the exigencies of modern life worldwide. Through this, this chapter invites readers to consider health and wellbeing beyond the narrow framework of biomedical models, and it pushes the reader to reconsider the centuries-old relationships between humanity and the natural world in the context of health and wellbeing. Across the globe, billions of people have lost touch with nature and the benefits it provides in their pursuit of materialistic desires and quick solutions to life's challenges. Unfortunately, this hurried and mechanical approach has increased health and wellbeing issues ranging from mental health issues to life-threatening illnesses. To overcome this, based on Hindu and Buddhist philosophical thought, this chapter attempts to provide evidence that solutions to health and wellbeing are within human reach. According to the great Indian saint Kabir Das, human happiness is found within, and seeking it in the outside world is futile. It further argues that it is possible to facilitate human beings becoming part of nature and, in turn, improve their health and wellbeing by utilizing secondary literature, case studies, and examples that even exist in modern lifestyles.

Chapter 5: Personal and Professional Encounters of Health and Wellbeing: Beyond Medical Sphere, is a personalized chapter with some biographical elements of the authors. This chapter provides their experiences with health and wellbeing, especially through growing-up and living in Sri Lanka and India. We point out that with the increased globalization and liberalization, traditional medical systems such as Ayurveda, Siddha, and Deshiya Chikitsa are becoming commercialized. In this context, nature and natural processes become less critical, and people may not receive the same benefits as the original form of herbs. It is essential to learn from ancient philosophies and systems by creating a battle of ideas so that we may be able to incorporate their valuable elements to deal with contemporary issues.

Chapter 6: The Conclusion revisits and answers the title question of this book: A new paradigm of health and wellbeing? This chapter presents a framework for different epistemologies to collaborate as equal partners to bring critical changes to improving health and wellbeing. We argue that biomedical interventions maintain short-term total health and wellbeing; however, insensitivities to nature and natural processes lead to recurring uncertainties and dangers. The traditional health systems, however, maintain a low level from an outside view and can facilitate sustainable health and wellbeing. Further, this chapter points towards the need for further research and policy changes as a conclusion.

References

Andrews, K. (2022). *The new age of empire: How racism and colonialism still rule the world*. Penguin.

Angus, I. (2016). *Facing the Anthropocene: Fossil capitalism and the crisis of the earth system*, New York: NYU Press.

Berry, H. L., Bowen, K., Kjellstrom, T., & Climate, A. C. (2018). Climate change and mental health: A causal pathways framework. *International Journal of Public Health, 63*(3), 327–337.

Bentham, J. (1970). In J. H. Burns, & H. L. A. Hart (Eds.), *An introduction to the principles of morals and legislation (1789)*. The Athlone Press.

Blume, H. (2006). Q&A with Arthur Kleinman. The Boston Globe. http://archive.boston.com/news/globe/ideas/articles/2006/07/23/qa_with_arthur_kleinman/. Retrieved on November 2, 2023.

Brennan, A., & Lo, Y. S. (2010). *Understanding environmental philosophy*. Routledge.

Cissé, G., R. McLeman, H. Adams, P. Aldunce, K. Bowen, D. Campbell-Lendrum, S. Clayton, K.L. Ebi, J. Hess, C. Huang, Q. Liu, G. McGregor, J. Semenza, and M.C. Tirado, (2022), Health, Wellbeing, and the Changing Structure of Communities. In H.-O. Pörtner, D. C. Roberts, M. Tignor, E. S. Poloczanska, K. Mintenbeck, A. Alegría, M. Craig, S. Langsdorf, S. Löschke, V. Möller, A. Okem, B. Rama (Eds.), *Climate change 2022: Impacts, adaptation and vulnerability*. Contribution of Working Group II to the Sixth Assessment Report of the Intergovernmental Panel on Climate Change (pp. 1041–1170). Cambridge University Press.

Das, V., & Han, C. (2015). *Living and dying in the contemporary world: A compendium*. University of California Press.

Datta, D. M. (1936). The Moral Conception of Nature in Indian Philosophy. *International Journal of Ethics, 46*(2), 223–228.

References

Davies, P. (2000). The relevance of systematic reviews to educational policy and practice. *Oxford Review of Education, 26*(3–4), 365–378.

De Silva, N., (2013), Sri Lanka's traditional knowledge and traditional cultural expressions of health and wellbeing: History, present status, and the need for safeguarding. In *SAARC Regional Seminar on Traditional Knowledge and Traditional Cultural Expressions in South Asia* (29–30).

Encyclopaedia Britannica. (2010). *Licchavi*, https://www.britannica.com/topic/Licchavi. Retrieved on May 18, 2024.

Fanon, F. (2005). *The wretched of the earth* (R. Philcox, Trans.). Grove Press.

Fadare, O. O., & Okoffo, E. D. (2020). Covid-19 face masks: A potential source of microplastic fibers in the environment. *The Science of the Total Environment, 737*, 140279.

Firth, J. (2020). *Science in medicine: When, how, and what*. Oxford University Press.

Foltz, R., & Saadi-nejad, M. (2008). Is zoroastrianism an ecological religion? *Journal for the Study of Religion, Nature and Culture, 1*(4), 413–430.

Frankopan, P. (2023). *The earth transformed: An untold history*. Bloomsbury.

Frierson, P., & Guyer, P. (2012). *Kant: Observations on the feeling of the beautiful and sublime and other writings*. Cambridge University Press.

Frawley, D., & Ranada, S. (1994). *Ayurveda: Nature's medicine*. Motilal Banarsidass.

Garro, L. C. (1990). Continuity and change: The interpretation of illness in an Anishinaabe (Ojibway) community. *Culture, Medicine, and Psychiatry, 14*(4), 417–454.

Green, B. N., Johnson, C. D., & Adams, A. (2006). Writing narrative literature reviews for peer-reviewed journals: Secrets of the trade. *Journal of Chiropractic Medicine, 15*(5), 5–19.

Haines, A., Ebi, K., Smith, K. R., Woodward, A., & Campbell-Lendrum, D. (2014), Climate change and human health: Impacts, vulnerability, and public health. *Public Health, 128*(3), 221–237.

Hayes, K., Blashki, G., Wiseman, J., et al. (2018). Climate change and mental health: Risks, impacts, and priority actions. *International Journal of Mental Health Systems, 12*(1), 28.

Illich, I. (1971). *Deschooling Society*, New York: Harper & Row.

Illich, I. (1973). *Tools of Conviviality*, New York: Harper & Row.

Jackson, D. W., & Riddlesperger, Jr. J. W. (2003). Thomas Jefferson and the rights of men (and women). In *Paper prepared for presentation at the Thomas Jefferson conference*. LSU.

Jadad, A. R., & O'Grady, L. (2008). How should health be defined. *BMJ, 337*, a2900.

Jaiswal, Y. S., & Williams, L. L. (2017). A glimpse of Ayurveda-The forgotten history and principles of Indian traditional medicine. *Journal of Traditional and Complementary Medicine, 7*(1), 50–53.

Jayawickrama, J. S. (2010). *Rethinking mental health and wellbeing interventions in disaster and conflict affected communities: Case studies from Sri Lanka, Sudan and Malawi* [PhD thesis, Northumbria University].

Jayawickrama, J. S. (2018). If you want to go fast, go alone. if you want to go far, go together: Outsiders learning from insiders in a humanitarian context. *Interdisciplinary Journal of Partnership Studies, 5*(2), 1–20.

Jayawickrama, J. S. (2023). Those who make an enemy of the earth make an enemy of themselves: Climate change and human activities from a South and Southeast Asian perspective. In D. Madhanagopal, & S. Momtaz (Eds.), *Climate change and risk in South and Southeast Asia: Socio-political perspectives*. Routledge.

Kaur, J. (1985). *The concept of man in Sikhism*. Gurmat Publishers.

Kleinman, A. (2006). *What really matters: Living a moral life amidst uncertainty and danger*. Oxford University Press.

Larson, J. S. (1999). The conceptualization of health. *Medical Care Research and Review, 56*, 123–136.

Lerner, H., & Berg, C. (2015). The concept of health in One Health and some practical implications for research and education: What is One Health? *Infection Ecology & Epidemiology, 5*, 25300.

Le Quéré, C., Jackson, R. B., Jones, M. W., Smith, A. J., Abernethy, S., Andrew, R. M., De-Gol, A. J., Willis, D. R., Shan, Y., Canadell, J. G., & Friedlingstein, P. (2020). Temporary reduction in daily global CO_2 emissions during the COVID-19 forced confinement. *Nature Climate Change, 10*(7), 647–653.

Levy, B. S., & Patz, J. A. (2015). Climate change, human rights, and social justice. *Annals of Global Health, 81*(3), 310–322.

Levitan, J., Carr-Chellman, D., & Carr-Chellman, A. (2017). Accidental ethnography: A method for practitioner-based education research. *Action Research,* 0(0), 1–17.

Macaulay, T. B. (1835). Minute by the Hon'ble T. B. Macaulay, dated the 2nd February 1835, Bureau of Education. In H. Sharp (Ed.), *Selections from educational records, Part I (1781–1839)* (pp. 107–117). Superintendent, Government Printing, 1920. Reprint. National Archives of India, 1965.

McMichael, A. (1993). Planetary overload: Global environmental change and the health of the human species. *Cambridge Quarterly of Healthcare Ethics, 2*(3), 282–296.

Mignolo, W. D. (2002). The geopolitics of knowledge and the colonial difference. *South Atlantic Quarterly, 101*(1), 57–95.

Mignolo, W. D. (2009). Epistemic disobedience, independent thought and decolonial freedom. *Theory, Culture & Society, 26*(7–8), 159–181.

Mignolo, W. D. (2011). *The darker side of Western modernity: Global futures, decolonial options.* Duke University Press.

Mignolo, W. D. (2021). *The politics of decolonial investigations.* Duke University Press.

Nandakumar, P. (1971). *Kamba Ramayanam. A condensed version in English verse and prose.* Sahitya Akademi.

Ngomane, M. (2019). *Everyday Ubuntu.* London: Transworld Publishers.

Nigosian, S. A. (1993). *The Zoroastrian faith: Tradition and modern research.* McGill-Queen's Press-MQUP.

Paniker, A. (2011). *Jainism: History.* Motilal Banarsidass Publishing House.

Patwardhan, B., Vaidya, A., & Chorghade, M. (2004). Ayurveda and natural product drug discovery. *Current Science, 86,* 789–799.

Paul, M. M., Greene, C. M., Newton-Dame, R., Thorpe, L. E., Perlman, S. E., McVeigh, K. H., & Gourevitch, M. N. (2015). The state of population health surveillance using electronic health records: A narrative review. *Population Health Management, 18*(3), 209–216.

Prata, J. C., Silva, A. L. P., Walker, T. R., Duarte, A. C., & Rocha-Santos, T. (2020). COVID-19 pandemic repercussions on the use and management of plastics. *Environmental Science & Technology, 54*(13), 7760–7765.

Quijano, A. (2000). Coloniality of power, eurocentrism, and Latin America. *International Sociology, 15*(2), 215–232.

Quijano, A. (2007). Coloniality and modernity/rationality. *Cultural Studies, 21*(2–3), 168–178.

Quijano, A., & Wallerstein, I. (1992). Americanity as a concept, or the Americas in the modern world-system. *International Journal of the Social Science, 134,* 549–557.

Radhakrishnan, S. (1939). *Eastern religions and western thought.* Galaxy Books.

Radhakrishnan, S. (1950). *The Dhammapada: With introductory essays.* Pali Text, English Translation and Notes. Oxford University Press.

Radhakrishnan, S. (1963). *Bhagavad Gita.* George Allen and Unwin Ltd.

Rainey, L. D. (2010). *Confucius & confucianism: The essentials.* Wiley-Blackwell.

Ramadan, A. M. H., & Ataallah, A. G. (2021). Are climate change and mental health correlated? *General Psychiatry, 34*(6), e100648.

Rodney, W. (1972). *How Europe Underdeveloped Africa,* London: Bogle-L'Ouverture Publications.

Sachs, W. (Ed.). (2010). *The development dictionary: A guide to knowledge as power* (2nd ed.). Zed Books.

Salminen, A., & Vadén, T. (2015). *Energy Experience: An Essay in Nafthology,* Dublin: MCM Publishing.

Saunders, J. (2000). The practice of clinical medicine as an art and as a science. *Medical Humanities, 26*(1), 18–22.

References

Smith, A. (1776). *An Inquiry into the Nature and Causes of the Wealth of Nations*. London: W. Strahan and T. Cadell.

Silva, B. M., Rodrigues, J. J., de la Torre Díez, I., López-Coronado, M., & Saleem, K. (2015). Mobile-health: A review of current state in 2015. *Journal of Biomedical Informatics, 56*, 265–272.

Sinclair, N. J. (2013). *Nindoodemag Bagijiganan A history of Anishinaabeg narrative*. The University of British Columbia.

Smith, L. T. (1999). *Decolonizing methodologies: Research and indigenous peoples*. Zed Books.

Smith, R. (2008). The end of disease and the beginning of health. *BMJ Group Blogs*. http://blogs.bmj.com/bmj/2008/07/08/richard-smith-the-end-of-disease-andthe-beginning-of-health/. Retrieved November 2, 2023.

Smith, N., & O'Keefe, P. (1980). Geography, Marx, and the concept of nature. *Antipode, 12*(2), 30–39.

Spiegel, P., Checchi, F., Colombo, S., & Paik, E. (2010). Health-care needs of people affected by conflict: Future trends and changing frameworks. *The Lancet, 375*(9711), 341–345.

Starr, S. F. (2012). *Lost Enlightenment: Central Asia's Golden Age*. Princeton University Press.

Subbarayappa, B. V. (1997). Siddha medicine: An overview. *The Lancet, 350*(9094), 1841–1844.

Sylvester, A., Tate, M., & Johnstone, D. (2013). Beyond synthesis: Re-presenting heterogeneous research literature. *Behaviour & Information Technology, 32*(12), 1199–1215.

Tao, C., Diao, G., & Cheng, B. (2021). The dynamic impact of the COVID-19 pandemic on air quality: The Beijing lessons. *International Journal of Environmental Research and Public Health, 18*(12), 6478.

Thapar, R. (2012). *Aśoka and the decline of the Mauryas* (3rd ed., p. 392). Oxford University Press.

UNDP. (2023). *Global multidimensional poverty index 2023: Unstacking global poverty: Data for high impact action*. United Nations Development Programme and Oxford Poverty and Human Development Initiative. https://hdr.undp.org/system/files/documents/hdp-document/2023mpire porten.pdf. Retrieved on December 27, 2023.

UNDP-OPHI. (2023). *Global multidimensional poverty index 2023—Unstacking global poverty: Data for high-impact action*. United Nations Development Programme and Oxford Poverty and Human Development Initiative.

Vale, M. M., Berenguer, E., Argollo de Menezes, M., Viveiros de Castro, E. B., Pugliese de Siqueira, L., & Portela, R. C. Q. (2021). The COVID-19 pandemic as an opportunity to weaken environmental protection in Brazil. *Biological Conservation, 255*, 108994.

Valtonen, A., Rantala, O., & Farah, P. D. (Eds.). (2020). *Ethics and Politics of Space for the Anthropocene*. Cheltenham: Edward Elgar Publishing.

WHO. (1948). *Constitution of the World Health Organisation*. International Health Conference.

WHO. (2021). *Climate change and health*. World Health Organization.

WHO. (2022). *World health statistics: Monitoring health for the SDGs*. World Health Organization.

Weiss, R. S. (2009). *Recipes for immortality: Healing, religion, and community in South India*. Oxford University Press.

White, B. P., Breakey, S., Brown, M. J., Smith, J. R., Tarbet, A., Nicholas, P. K., & Ros, A. M. V. (2023). Mental health impacts of climate change among vulnerable populations globally: An integrative review. *Annals of Global Health, 89*(1), 66.

Wignaraja, P. (1991). *Participatory development: Learning from South Asia*. United Nations University Press.

World Commission on Environment and Development. (1987). *Report of the world commission on environment and development: Our common future*. United Nations.

World Bank. (2022). *Poverty and shared prosperity 2022: Correcting course*. World Bank.

World Bank. (2023). *Population Data: South Asia*, https://data.worldbank.org/region/south-asia?view=chart, Retrieved on February 29, 2024.

Zelinsky, W. (1975). The Demigod's Dilemms. *Annals of the Association of American Geographers, 65*(2), 123–142.

Chapter 2
The Problem of Biomedical Definitions of Health and Wellbeing

2.1 Evolution of Health Concepts in Ancient Greek Philosophy and Medicine

> we will never eliminate pain;
> we will not cure all disorders;
> we will certainly die.
> Illich (1990, p. 8)

Medical practitioners, or physicians in the Hippocratic tradition, used to pledge to restore "health" or the balance of their patient's composition. However, they were forbidden to use their knowledge and skills to deal with death. There was an acceptance of nature's power to destroy the healing contract between the medical practitioner and their patient. A break with the Galenic-Hippocratic approach familiar to historians can characterize the idea of health and wellbeing within the European tradition. For Greek philosophers, health was a concept for harmonious blending—a balanced interplay of the basic elements. A person was healthy when they integrated themselves into the harmony of the totality of their world according to the place and time they had come into the world. Ancient Western philosophers, including Socrates, Antiphon, and Democritus, declared themselves as the physicians of the soul but not the body. In ancient philosophical terms, the disease of the soul refers not just to "mental disorders" as we label it in our modern psychiatry understanding but also to various internal obstacles to obtaining peace, a stable state of mind, melancholy, and different unwanted emotional dispositions. By labelling themselves as the physicians of the soul, it is understood that the ancient Western philosophers did not want to transgress into the fields of physicians and medical counterparts even though, in ancient times, philosophy and medicine heavily influenced each other. However, both fields usually stayed separate, with mutual respect for each other's expertise (Collins, 2007; Tountas, 2009).

2.1.1 Debates on the Body, Soul, and Disease

There have been contradictions among ancient Greek philosophers on the location of the source of human intelligence, including thoughts and emotions in the human body. Plato believed that the origin/site of man's intelligence is in the brain. On the other hand, Aristotle and the Stoics each posited arguments that the origin of human thoughts and emotions is in the heart. Alcmaeon and Hippocratic leaned towards the brain side. Such debates and early attempts on the origin/site of thoughts, emotions, and intelligence by the Green Philosophers carried through into the later philosophers, such as Praxagoras, Herophilus, and Galen. Galen, one of the most important physicians and philosophers of the later period, believed that philosophical accounts of the soul should be consistent with neurophysiology. This was because of experiments on live human subjects, and the dissection method emerged in the later centuries after Hippocrates and Herophilus. Ancient Greek philosophers and physicians generally possessed contrasting views on the causes of diseases, knowledge of the human body, and the integration of medicine and philosophy. Also, medical empiricists and dogmatists were the two schools of thought in ancient Greek medicine. The advocates of both of these schools played influential roles in the development of ancient Greek and Roman medicine—their influence extended into philosophy and science. The Medical Empiricists emphasized that it is through repeated practical experience, reports of others, and observation that medical theorems are generated; they rejected the view that science depends upon understanding the fundamental structures of things. Whereas the Dogmatists believed that trained physicians could and must find the fundamental causes of phenomena. Galen, a prominent figure in the field of medicine, sided with the Dogmatists and believed in the ability of scientists to uncover the deep causes of diseases through intelligence and application (Hankinson, 2003, p. 294–297).

As Tountas (2009) explained, despite the diverse and contrasting views that ancient Greek philosophers held on the various aspects of the human body and the causation of diseases, the ideas of balance, equilibrium, self-sufficiency, and harmony are firmly ingrained in ancient Greek philosophy, developed and expressed differently within their various cultures. For example, Pythagoras treated the human body's maladies and psychology with music's help (Babikian et al., 2013). Hippocrates, the father of Greek medicine, was known for playing music for his patients. Aristotle, another prominent philosopher, advocated music purifies emotions. The enthusiasm for music by the Greek philosophers as a type of medicine continued to grow later and remained influential in philosophy and music literature. This concept and discussion around using music as medicine and healing then influenced other traditions such as Arab, Chinese, and Indian. The translation of Greek writings on music into Syriac and Arabic also sparked discussions in early Islam about studying music's medical uses (Babikian et al., 2013; Shiloah, 1995, 2007). Overall, as discussed by Tountas (2009), this ancient Greek philosophy emphasized "empowerment" of people and communities through education and supportive environments, though it did not explicitly use the word "empowerment"; instead, these texts discussed the importance of humans to be freed from the shackles of superstitious beliefs and ignorance so that they can become self-sufficient, which in turn makes them independent rather than relying on others for their wellbeing. This idea of "self-sufficiency" aligned with empowerment, as individuals were encouraged to proactively take responsibility for their health and confront challenging external circumstances. In addition, the Pythagoreans, who promoted hygiene and emphasized the importance of maintaining perfect equilibrium, calmness, moderation, and self-control as fundamental elements of good health, had a significant influence on the development of medical science in the later Greek philosophy, particularly among the Hippocratic (Tountas, 2009). Old Greeks and Byzantine physicians and philosophers showed their attention towards nutrition and proper care during pregnancy, childbirth, and the neonatal period, too, as they were aware that these factors involved the health of not only the mother but the kid/s as well (Malamitsi-Puchner, 2021). Hippocrates acknowledged the importance of the mother's health in determining the child's health in the womb (Hanson, 1975).

2.1.2 "Harmony" and "Balance" Through the Ages

The concept of health as a harmonious blending and balanced interplay of the essential elements was emphasized by Greek philosophers (Sedley, 2003). They believed that people could achieve health by integrating themselves into the harmony of the totality of their world, taking into account the specific place and time they were born into. This idea of harmony and balance is deeply embedded in Greek philosophical understandings and reflected in various cultural settings. One example of applying this concept is using music as a therapeutic tool by the ancient Greek philosopher Pythagoras (Kulinski et al., 2022). Pythagoras argued that music could treat both bodily and psychological ailments. Further, he emphasized the importance of harmony in achieving health. Similarly, the Greek Philosopher Plato also contributed to understanding health as harmony. He believed that health is a state of complete harmony with the universe, emphasizing the interconnectedness of the individual with the larger cosmic order (van Wietmarschen et al., 2018).

2.1.3 Mental Disorders in Ancient European Philosophy

Marke Ahonen's book, "Mental Disorders in Ancient Philosophy," explores ancient philosophers' perspectives on mental disorders—a topic seldom discussed (Ahonen, 2014). She notes that mental disorders were frequently addressed in Greek and Roman mythology, incorporating mythological themes. However, ancient Western psychiatric thoughts, tracing back to Hippocrates, lacked an equivalent term for "mental disorder" in both Greek and Latin. Despite the absence of a specific term, ancient medical authors extensively examined what we now label as "mental disorders." Their understanding, distinct from modern psychiatric thoughts, attributed these disorders to bodily origins. Consequently, their treatment approach involved physical measures, even for conditions like melancholy.

Ahonen (2014) finds some rare instances in medical and non-medical texts of ancient Western philosophy that used the term "diseases of the soul." However, according to them, these "soul" related diseases are philosophical, and the philosophers are meant to handle them. Philosophers referred to these problems as more philosophical, moral, and analogous to bodily problems, as these mental disorders went against the natural order of things. Nevertheless, in this case, the philosophers, not the physicians, treat these disorders. By labelling themselves as the physicians of the soul, it is understood that the ancient Western philosophers did not want to transgress into the fields of physicians and medical counterparts. Despite the historical interplay between philosophy and medicine, these two fields generally maintained a respectful separation, each acknowledging the expertise of the other.

Here we clarify that discourses on harmony and balance were not just confined to ancient Greek philosophy. It was also recognized and discussed in other philosophical traditions as well. The Yijing, a Chinese philosophical text explored the idea of harmony and singularity—the universal concerns that philosophy addressed (Nelson, 2011). Harmony and balance are some of the central themes of ancient Indian Philosophical traditions. Vedas, Upanishads, Bhagavad Gita, Yoga Sutras of Hindu Philosophy, and ancient Buddhist and Jain texts emphasized the interconnectedness of all things in the Universe and advocated harmony and balance in human lives, and the importance of living by the natural order to achieve tranquillity and spiritual fulfilment (Easwaran, 1987; Gethin, 1998; Huchzermeyer & Zimmermann, 2002; Staal, 2008). Yoga Sutras of Patanjali advocated practices such as meditation, ethical living, and physical postures (exercise) as tools for attaining harmonious balance of mind and emotions (Satchidananda, 2012). In addition to philosophy, the concept of health as harmony was also discussed in various traditional medical systems of Asia, including Ayurveda and Siddha which will be discussed in the following portions of this book.

2.1.4 Medieval Views on "Natura": Divine to Rational Shift

As Draelants and Frunzeanu (2020) describe the concept of "natura" in the medieval period was complex, multifaceted, and evolved over the period. In the early medieval periods, "natura" encompassed the heavens, Earth, divine, and human environments. Whereas diverse views on "nature" gradually emerged in the long medieval millennium, the place, geographical factors, and intellectual conditions of their times influenced those divergent perspectives. The Middle Ages were when humans had limited influence and impact over nature, and the world's population was around two and four hundred million. During those periods, Western Christianity, which was rooted and centred over monasticism, was not perceived as a threat to the environment. Instead, the Biblical prescription orders humans to "go forth and multiply," which means encouraging humans to take forward the work that was started on the sixth day of Creation. It orders humans to take care of and be responsible for nature. The early medieval period was also where natural disasters, volcanic eruptions, and eclipses were often linked to famines, and they were perceived as a result of the punishments of Gods to humans. There was a major shift in the world views of Westerners towards "nature," particularly from the twelfth century onwards. There was a growing sense of logic and rational thinking in Western society. Historians attributed several reasons, including the relatively stable politics, resulting economic prosperity, and better yields and food productivity than the dark centuries of the medieval era. All these factors contributed to the thriving of urban centres, and urban schools became the centre of learning. The increasing sense of rationality in Western thoughts resulted in a new social role: the "intellectual" or "men of learning." Simultaneously, this intellectual curiosity also made humans view nature as the representative of God, responsible for the ongoing physical processes of Creation. This period is also known for the emergence of scholarly medicine, which marked the beginning of a more scientific and rational approach to studying the natural sciences, setting the stage for the development of natural sciences and the exploration of the Earth's terrestrial realm (Aberth, 2013; Draelants & Frunzeanu, 2019; Sorrell, 2009).

2.2 Health and Wellbeing in European Understanding: A Colonial Critical Overview

Sickness comes on horseback and departs on foot.

— A Dutch proverb

Like anywhere else, the European understanding of health and wellbeing has social, political, cultural, economic, and environmental contexts. Because of the colonial project, and since the establishment of global marketplace through the International Financial Institutions (IFIs) and the expansion of the capital marketplace through the neoliberal project, the European philosophies of the Enlightenment era had spread worldwide. As we write this book, the direct and indirect presence of European thought is looking over our South Asian shoulders. As argued by Dabashi (2015), the European knowledge construction is blind to other ways of thinking, does not have the ability to understand other cosmologies (or cosmovisions, as our Colombian friends would say), and can only epistemically paste what they already know upon the world. Various academic, scientific, and social definitions of health and wellbeing in non-European societies have been largely ignored in this process, and that is why it is essential to understand how Europeans developed an understanding of health and wellbeing within this context.

The most important aspect of examining the European philosophical and knowledge foundation is based on two elements. The first is the understanding of nature. The second is the understanding of the "Capital Landscape." Nature is the most examined concept in European natural and social sciences. Although understanding nature is fundamental to how European science perceives and operationalizes itself, nature is generally taken for granted (Smith & O'Keefe, 1980). Even in the contemporary discourse of mainstream knowledge, a deeper understanding of nature is lacking (Jayawickrama, 2023). Smith and O'Keefe (1980) further explain that the aim of the production of nature in the capital marketplace is to dominate nature—nature to be controlled, manipulated, and produced for its economic value rather than its fundamental worth. From this perspective, science, including biomedicine, has already become a commodity, and the sacredness of nature is of no economic value, as ancient civilizations understood. Therefore, it is abandoned for a rational pursuit. O'Keefe (2020) argued later in his career that this dualistic separation creates an understanding that life is external and not within oneself. In this external understanding, people continue to purchase commodities from the marketplace, mistakenly thinking that this constitutes living. This line of thinking, which flows from the Ancient Greeks to Rene Descartes to Adam Smith, and ultimately to linear scientific analysis and concepts of logical positivism, in other words, from mainstream knowledge systems, creates the contemporary worldview (Jayawickrama, 2023; Zelinsky, 1975). Further, Smith and O'Keefe (1980) point out that the positivist tradition dominates mainstream science, and this tradition inherently assumes that nature exists in and for itself, external to us and our activities. As stated succinctly, the result is a worldview in which the human population exists separately from nature. The worldview and understanding that emerged from Europe as we know today as mainstream knowledge evolved because of this process.

2.2.1 Perspectives of Malthus, Ricardo, Marx, and Rousseau

To understand the Capital Landscape the thoughts and contributions of four European thinkers should be heeded: Thomas Malthus (1766–1834), David Ricardo (1772–1823), Karl Marx (1818–1883), and Jean-Jacques Rousseau (1712–1778). Interestingly, they described the only way of falling off the cliff of capitalism or avoiding it. In a straightforward manner, Malthus wanted to preserve the power of the feudal aristocracy, and he wanted to finish with some of the more unacceptable traits of feudal agriculture but above all he sought to keep feudal power with the aristocracy. He welcomed the new bourgeoisie class but rejected their ascent as a political power. In that, Malthus, this new class was welcomed because they were the ones who led modern industrialization—the Western modernity. However, the goods it produced were for an aristocratic market that, after all, was the only group that could afford them. To firm up these arguments, Malthus developed a subset of arguments about the poor, the working class, who overbred and would forge a path to famine via self-over-population. This argument did not go down well with classes other than the feudal landlords. Ricardo and Marx shared an argument as both hated the feudal aristocracy, and both yearned for an end to feudalism and bonded labour. They saw the new industrial bourgeoisie, not tied to land, as revolutionary, making a range of necessary goods demanded by all. Where Ricardo and Marx disagreed was where the rewards of the new system, where the profits, should go. For Ricardo, the profits went to the new dominant economic and political class, the bourgeoisie, who took the risk. For Marx, the profits went to the people who generated them through surplus value extraction from their work, namely the emerging proletariat. As we can see, he positioned himself apart from the others, advocated for a rejection of both feudal and capitalist structures, and envisioned a contented peasantry free from feudal control. These four perspectives encapsulate the spectrum of political-economic analyses regarding the transition to a capitalist mode of production.

2.2.2 European Colonialism and Its Impacts on "Knowledge Systems"

To make a starting point in the European colonial history, we prefer to start from 1492, when Christopher Columbus "discovered" America—although he tried to discover India. In this, we consider 1492 as the beginning of the European philosophical and knowledge hegemony through the colonial project and expansion of the capital marketplace, including the spread of European knowledge. We highlight two flawed principles that have existed since the beginning. First, the Europeans labelled other civilizations as uncivilized and savage. Second, which emerged from the first, is the complete demotion of local populations, their wisdom, and expertise (Rodney, 1972). As Wignaraja (1991) argues, regardless of the colonial headquarters—the UK, France, Spain, Portugal, Belgium, or Germany—this was the standard policy of colonial administrations worldwide. People in colonies were constantly taught that the European knowledge systems were far superior to local wisdoms. Continued from this, Sen (1999) extends that these two flawed principles gave birth to two more sub-principles. The first was that European intellectuals invented the concepts of freedom and democracy. The advancement of equality of freedom and personal freedom was core to this idea. However, in inherent opposition to their own belief, none of the European Enlightenment philosophers supported the equality of freedom and personal freedom for women and slaves. The second was the rejection of teleology (six essences: earth, fire, wind, water, quintessential positive, and act of God) by the Enlightenment movement, which paved the way for modern science. Modern science understands the world through empirical methodology of knowledge acquisition by observation (through the five senses—seeing, hearing, tasting, smelling, and touching). This involves establishing hypotheses through induction based on observations of experiments and deduction to develop findings. In this process, the limitations of the human five senses were ignored, and anything beyond human understanding (or incapacity of understanding) was ignored as unscientific. Stated in terms of logical positivism, that which cannot be scientifically proven does not constitute knowledge. "The world is the totality of facts, not of things," as Wittgenstein states in the opening line of the Tractatus (Wittgenstein, 1921, 1.1).

2.2.3 Health and Wellbeing in Colonized Lands?

To pursue freedom ideals, the colonizers forcefully transformed colonies socially, culturally, economically, politically, and environmentally. For example, in 1561, Diego de Landa—the Spanish Bishop and Inquisitor—ordered all Mayan books to be collected and burned (Maestri, 2020). There are many similar exercises in colonial Asia, Africa, and the West Asia (Rodney, 1972; Tharoor, 2016). These annihilations not only prevented the advancement of local philosophies and knowledge systems but also systematically attacked the social, political, economic, cultural, and environmental systems of the colonies. Also, the people in the colonies were taught that their traditional and cultural wisdoms were unscientific and, therefore, useless. Missionary schools, universities, and higher education systems introduced in colonies methodically brainwashed generations to come. The elites and chosen youth from the colonies were given opportunities to study in colonial hubs, aiming to cultivate leaders bridging local and European perspectives. However, in return, their actions perpetuated the global division of human beings from nature through practices of expansion, growth, progress, and development (Wignaraja, 1991).

In the seventeenth-century Europe and North America, the shift towards mastering nature replaced the emphasis on people's health and wellbeing, and this transformation opened the door to cosmic health, suggesting the potential for engineering. Embracing the theory of engineerability, the notion of health as a possession gained widespread acceptance in the late eighteenth century. By the nineteenth century, it became common and prevalent among the masses to speak of "my health" and "my body." The US Declaration of Independence asserted the right to happiness (or wellbeing), and in a parallel manner, the right to health materialized. However, health has evolved into possessive individualism in contemporary understanding, legitimizing societies rooted in self-serving greed. From the seventeenth century onwards, colonial administrations forcefully disseminated Western biomedicine to the colonized nations through their imperial powers and trade settlements. Famous works such as "Curing Their Ills: Colonial Power and African Illness," and "Imperial Medicine and Indigenous Societies," extensively discussed how Western biomedicine was forcefully imposed on indigenous communities and how the emergence of Western medicine emerged as a hegemonic model in colonized nations by suppressing the plurality of native, indigenous, and traditional medicine and healing practices and philosophical systems (Arnold, 1988; Vaughan, 1991).[1]

---

[1] Literature on the colonial impact on nations in Asia has been extensive, and we will continue to discuss this throughout this book according to the context. Here, we shortly conclude these discussions and shift our focus to explore Western biomedicine's history and foundational concepts.

2.3 Understanding Western Biomedicine: Origins, Concepts, and Critiques

From Avicenna to Galen to Hippocrates to the European Renaissance, biomedicine approaches have evolved over centuries to become what we are experiencing today. They all made sense within the social, political, cultural, economic, and environmental contexts of their respective eras. In recent decades, Western biomedicine has been primarily based on empirical observation, experimentation, and inductive reasoning methods. Silvano (2021) traces the history of Western medicine and summarizes how it transformed over the past thousand years. As he writes, throughout the medieval period, there were continuous medical advancements in anatomy, surgery, and inventions in Europe, as well as the translation of medical writings from Asia to Europe and vice versa, resulting in the flow of medical knowledge among the regions. In the seventeenth century, a sudden and rapid transformation was driven by the emergence of microanatomists who began studying tissues.

Marcello Malpighi (1628–1694), an Italian Biologist and Physician, founded a new discipline, histology, which later became a central milestone in medical research. The seventeenth to nineteenth century was also the period where the entire Europe had to encounter the brutal effects of several epidemics—including exchange epidemics—where Europe exported diphtheria, measles, bubonic plague, smallpox, cholera, and more to the Americas and imported syphilis. Parallel to this, throughout the seventeenth and eighteenth centuries, hospitals in Europe became more and more specialized in pathology. Since then, several milestones occurred during this era in the history of Western biomedicine. A few of them are as follows: (i) Edward Jenner, an English physician and scientist, "invented" the vaccination procedure for treating smallpox, which became popular worldwide. (ii) Science and technology-driven surgery, anaesthesia techniques, and state-sponsored mass vaccination programmes played crucial roles in the nineteenth century, and the invention of the X-ray played a vital role in treating terminal illnesses such as cancer and skin diseases in the twentieth century. iii. As noted earlier, Western medicine became more and more specialized and was inclined more towards identifying germs through clinical examination and identifying vaccines to combat epidemics and life-threatening diseases throughout the eighteenth to twentieth centuries. The integration between clinical laboratories and hospitals became vital during this period.

As highlighted in the Stanford Encyclopedia of Philosophy, biomedicine is not merely a simple overlap between biology and medicine—in contrast, biomedicine refers to a philosophical framework that has a rich history and diverse philosophical commitments. Beyond this, this term implies a global institution biased towards Western culture and its power dynamics. In short, biomedicine primarily implies Western medical practices and their health infrastructure systems (Valles, 2020). Krieger (2011) traces the history of the term "biomedicine" and points that this term was used differently among countries in the nineteenth and twentieth centuries. The term "biomedicine" was first surfaced in the UK, and it became more popular in the public domain through the institute name "Institute for Biomedical Sciences," which was founded in 1912. Later, in 1943, this institute also started publishing "British Journal of Biomedical Sciences" which was again an important milestone of the widespread usage of the term "biomedical" and it largely implied laboratory-based authoritative scientific papers. Whereas in the USA, the terms "biomedicine" and "biomedical" are associated with basic and applied research, and it was primarily established by the federal government, in 1930, through the formation of National Institute of Health where the funds for research on the medical problems focusing on "biology" and "medicine" and in relation to each other (Harden, 2009; Krieger, 2011). Though the terms "biomedicine" and "biomedical" became increasingly popular in the twentieth century, it is still complicated to highlight what made a difference in the approach of doctors and scientists in both the nineteenth and twentieth centuries and is challenging to point out a single narrative in the changes of medicine. However, it is comparatively easier to implicate the changes in the approach of scientists and doctors with the war and post-war period (Lenoir & Hays, 2000). As Löwy (2011) argues that the World War II was a turning point in the biomedicalization process, in which there was a large-scale engagement and collaborations with the scientists, doctors, clinicians, industrialists, and the state—this was also seen as a continuum that happened in the wartime production of penicillin.

Krieger (2011) identifies that the terms "biomedicine" and "biomedical" are apparently similar in their meanings as they combine biological and medical concepts; even many dictionaries, including the Oxford English Dictionary (OED), do not differentiate them deeply. She lists the definitions provided by Oxford English Dictionary (OED), Medline Plus Medical Dictionary, WordNet, US National Institutes of Health, UK Institute of Biomedical Sciences (IBMS), On-line Medical Dictionary (OLMD), and National Research Council on biomedicine, biomedical, and biomedical models, and highlights the complexity among these definitions, and how it fails to capture all the aspects of biomedical approach. Notably, the historical influences of germ theory, hereditarian thinking, and eugenics, which have shaped the biomedical perspective, are visibly missing in these definitions.

Gaines and Davis-Floyd (2004) list the three essential features of biomedicine by referring to Gaines and Hahn (1985) and several other scholarly works. (i) Biomedicine is a distinct domain where it separates from other domains, and it possesses specialized knowledge and practices. (ii) Western biomedicine from other medicinal systems as it always attempts to disassociate from other domains including society, politics, religion, and economics[2]—which is uncommon with the other medicinal systems, including traditional medicines where it is still mostly associated with region, culture, and religion. (iii) Western biomedicine provides clear-cut roles, guidelines, and instructions to doctors, surgeons, clinicians, nurses, and almost all participants in its social and clinical encounters. These clear-cut roles and division of labour make it not only highly specialized but also highly hierarchical, which is complicated and multiple. According to Johnson (1985), the hierarchy in

---

[2] We argue that this statement may not be necessarily correct by showing how Western biomedicine was highly promoted by the state and integrated with other domains, including industry, economics, and politics.

biomedicine can be based on the nature of interventions. For example, surgeons who perform somatic interventions are typically more expensive than those who deal with psychological and mental issues. Another feature of Western biomedicine, which has received widespread critiques since the 1960s, has been its reductionist approach. In essence, Western biomedicine reduces diseases, illnesses, and treatment procedures to a biophysical phenomenon, restricting the study of diseases to only an experimental approach, primarily in lab settings.

Engel's (1977) scientific paper titled "The need for a new medical model: Challenge for biomedicine" is one of the influential works that details critiques against the biomedical model, particularly from the perspectives of psychiatric disorders. Some major critiques listed in this paper are as follows: (i) The biomedical model embraces the reductionist approach and mind–body dualism, that a complex phenomenon of human health and illnesses can only be understood and treated through physical and biochemical processes by neglecting the overall context of human nature. Also, the primary scientific emphasis of the biomedical approach is molecular biology, which again leads to the narrow focus on measurable biological variables to understand, identify, and treat diseases. (ii) It defines the "diseases" through somatic parameters by excluding social, psychological, and behavioural dimensions of illnesses. This approach makes physicians not concerned about the psychosocial issues of the patients as they lie outside the ambit of the responsibility of physicians (Engel, 1977; Fabrega, 1972; Krieger, 2011). (iii) Overall, Western biomedicine oversimplifies the complexity of disease, resulting in over-reliance on clinical and laboratory data. This finally results in diagnosing people who feel good as sick and vice versa. Historically, various cultural, social, and psychological dimensions have determined the contours between sickness and wellness. These dimensions are not adequately considered by the biomedical model, leading to reductionism and misinterpretation of disease, unnecessary hospitalization, overuse of drugs, misguided treatments, including surgery, and inappropriate tests (Engel, 1977; Holman, 1976).

As Engel writes (1977, p. 379),

> The dominant model of disease today is biomedical, with molecular biology its basic scientific discipline. It assumes disease to be fully accounted for by deviations from the norm of measurable biological (somatic) variables. It leaves no room within its framework for the social, psychological, and behavioral dimensions of illness. The biomedical model not only requires that disease be dealt with as an entity independent of social behavior, it also demands that behavioral aberrations be explained on the basis of disordered somatic (biochemical or neurophysiological) processes. Thus the biomedical model embraces both reductionism, the philosophic view that complex phenomena are ultimately derived from a single primary principle, and mind-body dualism, the doctrine that separates the mental from the somatic. Here the reductionistic primary principle is physicalistic; that is, it assumes that the language of chemistry and physics will ultimately suffice to explain biological phenomena…..

Critiques against Western biomedicine are not new. Scholars, including medical sociologists, anthropologists, and historians, have extensively discussed the loopholes and limitations of Western biomedicine over the past few decades. Interestingly, scholars from the West have also produced substantial works in this area. Despite the critiques, there have been several positive features of Western biomedicine, including understanding, treating, and preventing diseases systematically and its ability to provide coercive measures to treat sick individuals—it also developed taxonomies for the diseases, which led to the systematic understanding of many diseases which was unknown hitherto. Significantly, the Western biomedical model has contributed to the practical and advanced diagnostic tools and treatment procedures, including curing some cancers, significantly reducing the death rates of life-threatening illnesses, and providing immunization solutions to several epidemic diseases over the past few decades (Engel, 1977; Krieger, 2011).

Illich (1975), an Austrian philosopher, theologian, and social critic who puts radical views on health, education, and schooling, in his widely acclaimed book "Medical nemesis: the expropriation of health" argues how the modern (Western) medicine has become a nemesis or a force that threatens people to deprive their capacity to cope with their reality. He challenges conventional and exaggerated thoughts on modern medicine. He describes the multiple problems of Western Medicine, the gigantic creation of medical technology, and how it miserably fails to ensure people's health and wellbeing. Overall, this book identifies three aberrations or severe effects of modern medicine. They are (i) Clinical Iatrogenesis: Modern medicine has resulted in adverse drug reactions, medical errors, and multiple hospital-acquired infections, which Illich referred to as Clinical Iatrogenesis. (ii) Social Iatrogenesis: Modern medicine has provided absolute authority to the physicians to control human bodies, resulting in medical monopoly, over-reliance on medical professionals, and the healthcare systems becoming heavily standardized, which finally makes new categories of patients and categorizes certain people as unfit. Overall, when medicine affects not only individuals but also society as a whole and its functioning systems, it is referred to as Social Iatrogenesis. (iii) When medical systems redefine the concepts of pain, suffering, and pleasure that have culturally been embedded in society for generations and centuries, and make the society succumb before the authority of the medical and healthcare systems, and when the people lose their resilience to confront the reality, to embrace "sufferings" which is a part of the life, and fails to find the meaning of death, it is referred to as Cultural Iatrogenesis.

It is worth noting that Ivan Illich raised these questions even in the mid-twentieth century. In his book, he also counters many conventional thoughts that modern Western medicine has drastically dropped the mortality rate of many infectious diseases—for this, he puts forward the changing political and social landscapes, and the resulting hygienic practices were the primary reasons for the dropping of infectious diseases. However, he accepted that modern medicine effectively intervened in dealing with poliomyelitis and tuberculosis. Throughout the book, he raised concerns about how modern medicine trapped the entire humanity by replacing infectious diseases with modern epidemics such as coronary heart disease, diabetes, cancer, so-called mental disorders, and more. In the book, Illich does not focus only on health but also asks profound questions about the economic and technological advancement that happened in the twentieth century and how it continued to malnourish, under-nourish, and over-eating, sleepy sickness, and various other lifestyle-related disorders, and how it finally hit the health and wellbeing of humans—though this book mainly centres on developed economies such as USA and UK, the critiques that he points out on industrial expansion how discriminately hits the poor countries—for this, he provides examples from Latin American countries that a large portion of public taxes for medical education and public health are being passed to build the lavish private hospitals and these hospitals provide absolute autonomy to the physicians, finally resulted in medical monopoly and the control of the body of humans.

In an industrial society, medical intervention does not change the prevailing image of health and death but caters to it. It diffuses the death image of the medicalized elite among the masses and reproduces it for future generations. However, when "death prevention" is applied outside of a cultural context in which consumers religiously prepare themselves for hospital deaths, the growth of hospital-based medicine inevitably constitutes a form of imperialist intervention. A sociopolitical image of death is imposed; people are deprived of their traditional vision of what constitutes health and death. The self-image that gives cohesion to their culture is dissolved, and atomized individuals can now be incorporated into an international mass of highly "socialized" health consumers. The expectation of medicalized death hooks the rich on unlimited insurance payments and lures the poor into a gilded death trap (Illich, 1975, p. 76). In such an intensely industrialized society, people are conditioned to get things rather than do them; they are trained to value what can be purchased rather than what they can create. They want to be taught, moved, treated, or guided rather than learn, heal, and find their own way. Impersonal institutions are assigned personal functions. Healing ceases to be considered a task for the sick. It first becomes the duty of the individual body repairmen and then soon changes from a personal service into the output of an anonymous agency. In the process, society is rearranged for the sake of the healthcare system, and it becomes increasingly difficult to care for one's own health. Goods and services litter the domains of freedom (Illich, 1975, p. 80).

2.4 Biomedicine Within the Dominant Epistemology

Following through the arguments established by Mignolo (2009, 2012), biomedicine is based on inductive and deductive scientific approaches. While this epistemological approach is native to Europe and somewhat to the North American European population, there are many different epistemological approaches in the rest of the world. However, it is now well established in medical anthropology that there is no universal biomedicine, but heterogeneous forms of biomedical technologies and interventions. What they share, at least to some degree, and that makes them biomedical, is presumed hegemonic status because their conclusions about, definitions of, and responses to disease that are legitimated (and sometimes challenged) by official scientific knowledge, that is, biology, chemistry (in pharmaceuticals), and visual representations of anomalies in the body. This shift in global health also signifies significant changes in biomedical enterprises. Biomedical forms of knowledge and practice have long been enrolled in empire and nation-building projects. We are currently in the midst of a "longer wave of biomedical globalization, carried out by development agencies, NGOs, and other humanitarian efforts to improve the health of the global poor. A nascent biomedical technology market that provides services and goods to those who can afford to pay for them also promotes this last phase" which might be referred to as a "non-governmental" phase (Lock & Nguyen 2018, p.148). While there is no universal biomedicine, there is however, a "universal" scientific foundation to biomedicine, which is based on European epistemology. This has created an epistemological injustice in defining health and wellbeing within a dominant epistemology.

2.5 Ancient Versus Modern Views on Body and Health

In the modern world, more and more lives are lost to disasters, conflicts, technological hazards, and uneven development. Those in less privileged situations often become unwitting victims of medical interventions, akin to the escalating use of medicine mirroring the fast-food trend. Against this backdrop, examining the conventional biomedical definitions of health and wellbeing is crucial. In his pseudonymous work on Hatha Yoga, William Walker Atkinson (1862–1932) elaborates on the fundamental differences between the Yogic philosophy and Western physical enthusiasts' approach towards the body. In ancient Hindu Philosophy, Yogis believes that the real human is not merely their physical body. Instead, they believe that humans feel that the part of their body feels immortal, often referred to as "I," which is not a mere body of fleshy nature but something more profound. Despite this deep understanding, Yogis also recognizes that the body should be cared for and nurtured correctly to achieve the great parts of man. Hence, Yogis do not relinquish the importance of keeping the body strong and healthy. They went beyond and emphasized that the body should be in control of the mind, tuned to respond to the guidance of the spirit. The body must first be strong and healthy to achieve this level of responsiveness. That is why the Yogis greatly emphasizes bodily health and physical wellbeing. This fundamentally differs from Western physical culture, where the body is often equated with the physical strength and appearance. Yogis control and master their bodies voluntarily and involuntarily, which Western physical enthusiasts are unfamiliar with (Ramacharaka, 1904). According to Plato, health was a bodily quality, and spiritual health, too, a quality. The German language term, "Gesundes menschliches Verständnis"—healthy human understanding, regardless of critiques by Kant, Hamann, Hegel, and Nietzsche, preserved something of this idea.

Similarly, the medical practitioners and physicians in Ancient Asia, Africa, West Asia, and many other civilizations practised with care and compassion towards patients. Of course, they were not practicing medicine in the contemporary capital marketplace. The boundaries between nature and human beings have been eliminated in the contemporary world. Since the beginning of the twentieth century, the physician has become an appointed instructor of societies where patients have lost their competence. Medical students today are learning to consider themselves responsible for the lives of people from the womb, and their success is measured in the form not only treating diseases, but even "treating" old age where people continue to live longer. The modern biomedicine has encroached unescapably into the sanctuary of human being. From mapping DNA and genetic cleansing; embryo cloning; and organ transplants are all attempts to "prevent" death.

2.5.1 Biomedical Definitions of "Health" and "Wellbeing" Through a Critical Lens

Revisiting with the discussions made in the previous chapter, considering that the World Health Organization (WHO) is the leading authority on health in the global platform, their definition of health has a major impact on the world's population. World Health Organization (1948), "a state of complete physical, mental, and social wellbeing and not merely the absence of disease or infirmity." We agree that when this definition was developed, it represented a groundbreaking idea according to the global political, social, and economic context of its period. The definition was remarkably ambitious as it encompassed the physical, mental, and social domains of health. However, since then, there have been numerous rapid transformations have occurred in different spheres—global and local contexts have evolved and continued to change. Population dynamics are shifting, and the prevalence of technological and natural hazards is giving rise to various diseases and illnesses. The climate change crisis is altering pathogen life cycles, impacting the ability of animals, including humans, to cope with different types of pathogens and generally influencing the physical, mental, and social conditions of people. Despite all these significant changes, the definition of health established in 1946 has remained unaltered and has not adapted to evolving contexts.

The primary criticism directed at the WHO definition is its expectation of completeness in the physical, mental, and social wellbeing of individuals. This notion implies that almost all of us must be experiencing some form of physical, mental, or social illness or disease. However, a fundamental problem arises from the fact that biomedical definitions are subject to constant change, often influenced by economic and financial considerations and, in some cases, pressure from pharmaceutical companies. For example, according to James et al. (2014), in 1982, the definition of hypertension worldwide blood pressure was 160/100 mmHg or above, and in 2014, it became 150/90 mmHg or above in the USA and 140/90 mmHg or above in the UK.

In a personal discussion with a medical academic in Sri Lanka in 2023, it was revealed that Sri Lanka transitioned its definition of hypertension for blood pressure from the US to the UK standard. The shift was driven by the impracticality of the US definition, which categorized over half of the Sri Lankan adult population as hypertensive, posing challenges for a developing nation. Adopting the UK definition reduced the rate to a more manageable 30% of the adult population of Sri Lanka. We highlight this anecdote as it underscores the impracticability and lack of measurability of the idea of completeness in the WHO definition of health. During the ascendancy of biomedical models in the nineteenth and early twentieth centuries, diseases took centre stage, with an average life expectancy of 47 years. In the contemporary world, particularly in Europe and North America, the average life expectancy has risen to 74 years, shifting the focus to chronic illnesses and non-disease-specific complaints (Kinsella & Velkoff, 2001; Woodwell, 1999). This focus on disease and illness, due to changing social, political, cultural, economic, and environmental contexts, as well as changing health needs, leads to undertreatment, overtreatment, and mistreatment (Tinetti & Fried, 2004). Further, Tinetti and Fried (2004) argue that the biomedical model is delivered when the patients meet the criteria, physicians are hesitant to treat patients who do not meet the accepted diagnostic criterion, which leads to undertreatment. A 40-year-old man in Sri Lanka complained to a physician about severe back pains, with difficulties in breathing, eating, and sleeping. Because the physician is a cardiologist, he could not find any problems with the heart of the patient. Many patients come to hospitals with complaints that cannot be understood within a linear examination or analysis. Tinetti and Fried (2004) also argued that the importance of preventing and treating individual diseases and illnesses leads to overtreatment, often with adverse effects. A 92-year-old woman in the UK was diagnosed with Type 2 diabetes. The diabetic specialist cut down all her sugar intake with a prescription of metformin. The nutritionist advised her to stop taking a glass of Sherry in the evenings as she has been doing that for the past 70 years. After the treatments started, within six months, the older woman died. Regarding mistreatment, Tinetti and Fried (2004) point out that clinical decision-making is based on the outcomes rather than patient preferences. While useful in many instances, the disease or illness-based specializations of doctors, nurses, and hospitals can be detrimental in other instances. Finally, what is striking is that Cunningham et al. (2008) found that when physicians go on strike, mortality is either not affected or decreases, and can be interpreted as that doctors have very little influence and impact on mortality. They analysed five strikes between 1976 and 2003 worldwide to produce this research outcome.

2.5.2 Normalization and Correction: Biomedical Definitions Within the Capital Marketplace

According to the Marriam-Webster Dictionary (2023), the word "normal" came to English around the seventeenth century, from the Latin normalis, which means "made according to a carpenter's square, forming a right angle." This "right angle" sense was among the earliest of those applied to normal in English. What is considered "normal" determines clinical medicine practice and has implications at an individual level, doctor-patient relationship, and health care policies. With the increase in medical information and technical abilities, examining this concept of normality in medicine is essential so that crucial discussions can be held unequivocal. Example: Adolphe Quetelet's development of BMI based on astronomy and mathematics. This idea of

BMI appealed to life insurance companies, which created "ideal" weight tables after the turn of the century. By the 1970s and 1980s, the measurement, now dubbed body mass index, was adopted to screen for and track obesity. Now, it is everywhere, using an equation—essentially a ratio of mass to height—to categorize patients as overweight, underweight, or at a healthy weight. It is appealingly simple, with a scale that designates adults who score between 18.5 and 24.9 as within a healthy range. Some health determinants include socializing, community involvement, exercise levels, access to healthcare, satisfaction with life, housing, friendships, and financial security, which is beyond a simple measurement of physical self of a person. However, it is interesting to note that substantial human health and wellbeing research conducted in North America emphasized the higher quality of living, exclusive of the discussions of nature. On the other hand, most studies that centre on the links between health and nature do not focus on the natural world itself but instead on the "environment" and "pollution" (Basu & Lanphear, 2019; Evers et al., 2022; O'Connor et al., 2008).

2.6 Discussing Health and Wellbeing Minus "Nature": Is It Feasible?

Discussing health and wellbeing without considering nature and its exploitation and the ways in which modern societies continue to live since industrialization era raises serious concerns about the holistic understanding of human wellness. However, in most discussions on Western biomedicine related to medical, pharmaceuticals, or health, nature is either overlooked or not given enough attention. In a few cases, discussions on the environment replace nature. In reality, our contemporary societies continue to consume more and more resources due to material development, the promotion of selfishness, exploitation, and profits. The violent and competitive nature of day-to-day life, including travel, work, education, and relationships, has created more and more stressors for people (Prashad, in Podur, 2022), and it has already had adverse repercussions on health and wellbeing of billions, and in the future, it will continue to rise without any doubt. This makes human beings incapable of dealing with life itself (including health and wellbeing) and harms the environment and planet. The general message that runs through capitalistic societies is that people need to work hard to support the marketplace and profits, to make a living, and to save enough to live happily as consumers in retirement. This narrative is not enough, as the pursuit of greed leads exclusion and never-ending consumption, resulting in we, humans, do not have time to think about nature. When we look around contemporary societies, narratives of growth, progress, winning, or victory are prominent. Modern societies are filled with celebrities in the entertainment industry, academia, politics, sciences, and many other fields. This is, in large part, due to the revolutionized communication through the mobile technology of today. Attached to this comes the products for sale—promoting everlasting consumerism and ubiquitous advertisements for further consumption. Two processes are emerging: first, people's imagination and creativity are being destroyed because they fail to serve an economic purpose in the capital marketplace, and second, people believe without inquiry.

In many ways, scholars such as Illich (1971), Bush and Saltarelli (2000), and Smith (2000) commented on the repetitive nature and problems with systems of contemporary knowledge transference to students in the form of information without critical examination in mainstream education. There is increasing information flow, but Smith (2000) explains that contemporary universities have become corporate organizations in most countries. While traditional education aims to train the future labour force, contemporary education has become profitable (Smith, 2000). In this, any intellectual debate, scientific inquiry, or general responsibility towards society or nature is controlled by financial benefits. Illich (1973) predicted that instead of facilitating analytical thinking within students, this type of education produces frustration, hatred, self-indulgence, and greed. In return, this process takes out the joy of life and living.

In day-to-day life, we buy materials because they are advertised as important or improve the quality of life. However, do we examine and critically evaluate the information transferred into our heads? Do we even question what damage is being done to the natural world around us, within us? Suppose humans are to protect the environment or live harmoniously with nature. In that case, we need this critical thinking and questioning as "the Light of Asia" Buddha suggested (Henning, 2002). The risk of believing what is presented to us through various information channels, including educational institutions, is that we easily end up in arrogance, which leads to hatred, self-indulgence, and greed.

Contemporary mainstream knowledge results in compartmentalization, a division of knowledge, because of Adam Smith's division of labour (Smith, 1776). For example, this compartmentalized learning, and treatments govern institutional education and health systems (Illich, 1978). Education is delivered in a classroom by a trained professional, and health has become specified and is delivered only by a specialist (Illich, 1971). While there is a usefulness in the specialism, this also creates a disconnection. This notion of division or compartmentalization is promoted within societies as an achievement or self-made (Ngomane, 2019). This idea of achievement is so dominant within societies that the individual becomes self-centred and completely overlooks the connection to other human beings, animals, trees, and the entire planet. Grades, qualifications, and status as power and quality of knowledge become linked to the position, and pursuits are only worthy if they serve some form of economic or personal gain. As a result, industrialization, technological advances, conquering, and colonial ideologies continue sweeping the contemporary world. Taming rivers, breaking prairies, clearing forests, and claiming the earth for the benefit of humans have become a common theme in many development projects over the years. These self-destructive and earth-ravaging approaches to life and living will not suffice for humans to survive. A shift in worldview, a shift in perspective, and relationship to nature is needed. Smith and O'Keefe (1980), over 40 years ago, understood this problem. They argued that production in the capital marketplace cannot continue without the production of nature and, as a by-product, space. However, due to the conflict, ambiguous and unconscious process of controlling nature, what

Smith and O'Keefe (1980) found as the production of nature results in destruction. O'Keefe (2020) argued against dualism, the destruction of nature, and capitalist acts of collection that disregard nature while calling for a critical examination of the human and nature relationship in all aspects of our livelihood in pursuit of effective change.

2.6.1 From Typhus to COVID-19: Tracing Medical Sociology Through the Lens of Politics, Media, and Health Narratives

> Medicine is a social science and politics is nothing else but medicine on a large scale. Medicine as a social science, as the science of human beings, has the obligation to point out problems and to attempt their theoretical solution; the politician, the practical anthropologist, must find the means for their actual solution.
>
> Virchow (1848) (Original was in German)

In early 1848, a 26-year-old young man, Rudolf Virchow, made an official trip to Upper Silesia as an external expert to the economically depressed Polish minority region within Prussia to assess the impacts of Typhus Epidemic, which intensified the potential scandal. Virchow was a junior lecturer in pathology at the Charité Hospital in Berlin and he spent only three weeks in Upper Silesia from the end of February 1848 to early March 1848, and produced a highly influential report entitled "Mittheilungen über die in Oberschlesien herrschenden Typhus-Epidemie" in 1848 (Virchow, 1848—excerpts of English translation from this report, Virchow, 2006). In this report, he argues the ways in which corrupted bureaucracy, aristocracy, plutocracy, and political oppression had deprived the Upper Silesian people for decades, and how it resulted in famine, which further led to crop failures over the years. All these effects affected only the poor Polish peasants, but not other powerful stakeholders. Continuous oppression over the years and decades had made these people accept the brunt of famine, epidemics, scandals, and even death silently and painfully. Ultimately, he concluded that the causes of the epidemic are "social," and the root cause is "political." Given this, he argued that the necessary response to the epidemic lies in "political" rather than "medical" solutions (Mackenbach, 2009; Taylor & Rieger, 1985).

Bloom (2002) points out another influential physician of the eighteenth century, Salomon Neumann, who studied the links between socioeconomic factors, including poverty and occupation, with health and wellbeing and famous for his works on medical statistics in the Prussian state, shared Virchow's view. However, as clarified by Bloom, the perspectives of Virchow and Neumann on "Social Science" were highly different than what we refer to as "Social Science" in our contemporary understanding. According to them, "social science" was a practical, advocacy-driven field closely tied to political action, partisanship, and the pursuit of social reform. Despite the influential works by Virchow and Neumann linking the socioeconomic and political factors with health and wellbeing, there were no big academic interests shown to develop the theoretical constructs and cumulative research in this field, resulting in "medical sociology" as an independent academic discipline had not emerged until the early twentieth century. In this context, it is also important to highlight that the "sociology" was not well established before the mid of the nineteenth century. This period was characterized by the Industrial Revolution and the growing influence of enlightenment values, and the concept of the "right to health" was becoming increasingly popular in the Western nations. Hence, the fields "medicine" and "sociology" often intermingled with a strong focus on politics and social reform, and the roles and responsibilities of physicians and medical sociologists became more specialized over time. The concept of a physician as a public benefactor was fully expressed only in the nineteenth century. Also, in the middle of the nineteenth century, Western societies started recognizing the adverse consequences of industrialism, and economic liberalization's grip slowly weakened. During this period, the terms "public health," "social hygiene," and "social medicine" were often used interchangeably, and there was a conspicuous absence of a theoretical framework to approach the issue of public health in a methodical and organized manner. Hence, historical trajectory of medical sociology of nineteenth century was marked by a dynamic interplay between medicine, social sciences, and advocacy.

In the early 1990s, social medicine experienced a revival—one of the prominent contributors to social medicine was Alfred Grotjahn, a German physician and social hygienist (Willich & Berghöfer, 2013). The discipline of medical sociology slowly got shaped and emerged from Social Work in the USA and social hygiene efforts in Europe and England. The universities in the USA have played a more prominent role in shaping this discipline in an organized manner, although universities in England and Germany have also made significant contributions. The timeline of modern medical sociology begins in 1940 and extends to the present day. This period marks the emergence of medical sociology as a visible field within general sociology. The process of becoming a recognized specialty was initiated during this time, with various factors and patterns of development influencing its growth. World War II played a significant role in establishing the role of sociology in national affairs, like how the discipline of psychology emerged during the First World War (Hollingshead, 1973). The period from 1945 to 1960 was marked by the training of young scholars who would become leaders in medical sociology. Since 1980, medical sociology has faced challenges to its intellectual and institutional identity, including a contraction of federal support for the social sciences and increased competition from other disciplines. However, medical sociology in the USA still enjoys a prominent status compared to other nations worldwide (Bloom, 2002; Pescosolido & Kronenfeld, 1995).

2.6.2 Media, Politics, and Public Health: Where Are the Links?

In many world regions, things around epidemics have not changed much even after 150 years, but they happen in different forms. For example, Surat in Gujarat, India, faced a Plague outbreak 1994. The nature and causes of the epidemic in this city were undefined, and multiple reasons were attributed. Politics played a major role in intensifying this public health crisis as the powerful institutions and authorities, such as the World Health Organization (WHO), the Union Government of India, and the state government of Gujarat, had differing priorities and perceptions of the outbreak (Sivaramakrishnan, 2011). Compared to the Typhus Epidemic in Upper Silesia, the Plague epidemic in Surat received international attention thanks to dramatic coverage by International and regional media outlets. Also, during the Typhus Epidemic, Virchow visited Upper Silesia as an external expert under the invitation of the Prussian Government.

Meanwhile, during the plague epidemic in 1994, the WHO team visited India, including Surat, the affected city. Initially resistant to external interventions, the Union government of India later succumbed to pressures from international media outlets, neighbouring nations, and trade partners. However, the state government of Gujarat remained resistant and critical of the Union government's centralized approach in responding to the epidemic, initially denying that the outbreak was the plague. This created confusion and scepticism among the public, further intensifying the public health crisis. Thus, social anxieties, politics, and media dramatization played pivotal roles in shaping the response to this epidemic (Lin, 1995; Sivaramakrishnan, 2011). Sivaramakrishnan (2011) argued that politics played a major role in intensifying the public health crisis during the Surat Plague Outbreak. Different institutions and authorities, such as the World Health Organization (WHO), the central government of India, and the state government of Gujarat, had differing priorities and perceptions of the outbreak. This led to debates and conflicts over the nature of the disease and its origin, delaying the implementation of effective measures to control the outbreak.

Similarly, Lin (1995) traced how the international media outlets dramatically covered the Plague epidemic not as a public health concern but as a media opportunity. He highlighted the international press reports, including the prominent New York Times, which carried the front-page coverage of not just the news of the Plague epidemic but also the mass exodus of around 0.2 million people from Surat city, which was the epicentre of this disease. Also, it was presented in the way that the plague suddenly recurred in Surat, which had been vanquished from the world earlier—whereas the truth was otherwise. Just around a month back then, in August 1994, the outbreak of the Bubonic Plague was reported in 25 villages of the neighbouring state, Maharashtra, with around 90 cases, but no deaths were reported. Eighty children died in June 1995 in Muzzafarpur, Bihar, due to encephalitis. Both these events were unnoticed by the international media, so no panic had happened.

Roughly twenty-five years later, the world was gripped by the COVID-19 pandemic for about two years. Again, politics came to the fore in responding to this health crisis. Politics played an integral role in the entire trajectory of COVID-19, from the initial announcement of the virus to acknowledging the pandemic, implementing measures like shutdowns, preparing and distributing vaccines, and even utilizing the virus as a strategy to stifle local voices and supporting crony capitalism (Byttebier, 2022; Greer et al., 2021; Sabahelzain, 2021).

While health and wellbeing were once believable ideals in the nineteenth and early twentieth centuries, today, they represent elements of a lost past with no return. These normative notions no longer provide meaningful guidance to individuals. Attempts to structure lives around these ideals can be damaging, leading to self-induced sickness. In the contemporary world, capitalism, dominated by neoliberalism and marketplace fundamentalism, encourages a culture of self-serving greed and commodifying health. Global governance—shaped by governments and various national and international institutions—operates through austerity programmes, pharmaceutical and food management, trade and investment governance, and rules facilitating globalized manufacturing and consumerism (Sell & Williams, 2020). The COVID-19 pandemic exposed the increasing health crises in the developing world and the developed world because health and healthcare are located within the capital marketplace. Privatization of health care, reduction of financial and resource allocation for public sector institutions, and public subsidization of private profit-making through the transfer of income tax into private insurance companies have worsened the health of populations (Waitzkin, 2020). Global capitalism, which has emerged through European philosophical thinking and advanced by North American thought and practice, has become a sociostructural institution in the everyday lives of many people worldwide. Therefore, scholars such as Flynn (2021) argue that global capitalism must be considered a health determinant.

To take these arguments into personal account, the first author's father was born into the British colony of Ceylon in 1931. In 1937, he was enrolled in a Catholic school in his village. He remembered how he was beaten up from day one for speaking in Sinhala, his native language, in the school. He was taught that the European ways of dressing, eating, and behaviour are what a gentleman should follow. Further, he was taught that being a farmer, traditional medical practitioner, or merchant was not acceptable in a civilized society. Although he came from a rural family, he never learned about the wonders of nature or farming or had the opportunity to learn traditional Sri Lankan scriptures. In these approaches, contemporary Sri Lankan society does not value traditional medical approaches (*Deshiya Chikitsa*) as much as biomedicine.

If we view global capitalism as a determinant of health, it becomes easier to understand concepts of health and wellbeing within Euro-centric philosophies. Countries such as the USA and the UK in the Global North, as well as most South Asian countries in the Global South, indicate that poor health is strongly linked to poverty. In her popular commentary, "Is US Health the Best in the World?" Starfield (2000) pointed out that the nature and operation of the healthcare system, the relationship between error and non-error adverse effects and the type of care received, and the relationships among income inequality (poverty), social disadvantage, and characteristics of health systems, including primary and specialty care, all provide the basis for considering neglected factors. The European Enlightenment claims freedoms, which are strongly associated with the capitalist marketplace because it is believed to ensure moral self-responsibility. Machan (1986) points out two types of freedoms within this idea—positive and negative. What is missing here is that attraction, false belief, impulse, desire, hardship, or ill health are all beyond these freedoms because most of the world population has no control over the capital marketplace. In the capital marketplace, the manufacturing that produces profit for the capitalist does not facilitate the health of the workers, who are much of the population of any society (Das, 2023).

Revisiting the entire chapter, our effort has been to provide pointers towards the disjuncture between humans and nature, and how this has created more and more health and wellbeing challenges. Through scientific methodology, humans have become external to nature, while drawing resources from the environment (Smith & O'Keefe, 1980). This dichotomous positionality is not only destroying the health and wellbeing of human populations, but the planet we live on. The biomedical model, while capable of maintaining a long life, is insufficient to facilitate a quality of life with overall health and wellbeing of human populations due to the limitations of scientific analysis.

References

Aberth, J. (2013). *An environmental history of the middle ages: The crucible of nature.* Routledge.
Ahonen, M. (2014). *Mental disorders in ancient philosophy.* Springer.
Arnold, D. (Ed.). (1988). *Imperial medicine and indigenous societies* (Vol. 6). Manchester University Press.
Babikian, T., Zeltzer, L., Tachdjian, V., Henry, L., Javanfard, E., Tucci, L., et al. (2013). Music as medicine: A review and historical perspective. *Alternative and Complementary Therapies, 19,* 251–254.
Basu, N., & Lanphear, B. P. (2019). The challenge of pollution and health in Canada. *Canadian Journal of Public Health, 110,* 159–164.
Bloom, S. (2002). *The word as scalpel: A history of medical sociology.* Oxford University Press.
Bush, K. D., & Saltarelli, D. (2000). *The Two Faces of Education in Ethnic Conflict: Towards a Peacebuilding Education for Children, Innocenti Insight.* United Nations Publications.
Byttebier, K. (2022). *COVID-19 and capitalism: Success and failure of the legal methods for dealing with a pandemic.* Springer Nature.
Collins, M. (2007). Healing and the soul: Finding the future in the past. *Spirituality and Health International, 8*(1), 31–38.
Cunningham, S. A., Mitchell, K., Narayan, K. V., & Yusuf, S. (2008). Doctors' strikes and mortality: A review. *Social Science & Medicine, 67*(11), 1784–1788.
Dabashi, H. (2015). *Can Non-Europeans think?* Zed Books.
Das, R. J. (2023). Capital, capitalism and health. *Critical Sociology, 49*(3), 395–414.

Draelants, I., & Frunzeanu, E. (2020). Creation, generation, force, motion and habit: Medieval theoretical definitions of nature. *Making sense of health, disease, and the environment in cross-cultural history: The Arabic-Islamic world, China, Europe, and North America* (pp. 27–60). Springer International Publishing.

Easwaran, E. (1987). *The Upanishads*. Nilgiri Press.

Engel, G. L. (1977). The need for a new medical model: A challenge for biomedicine. *Science* (New York, N.Y.), 196(4286), 129–136.

Evers, C., & Phoenix, C. (2022). Relationships between recreation and pollution when striving for wellbeing in blue spaces. *International Journal of Environmental Research and Public Health, 19*(7), 4170.

Fabrega, H., Jr. (1972). The study of disease in relation to culture. *Behavioral Science, 17*(2), 183–203.

Flynn, M. B. (2021). Global capitalism as a societal determinant of health: A conceptual framework. *Social Science & Medicine, 268*, 113530.

Gaines, A. D., & Davis-Floyd, R. (2004). Biomedicine. In C. R. Ember, & M. Ember (Eds.), *Encyclopedia of medical anthropology*, 1, pp. 95–109.

Gaines, A. D., & Hahn, R. A. (1985). Among the physicians: Encounter, exchange and transformation. In R. A. Hahn, & A. D. Gaines (Eds.), *Physicians of western medicine: Culture, illness and healing*, 6, pp. 1–25.

Gethin, R. (1998). *The foundations of Buddhism*. Oxford University Press.

Greer, S. L., King, E., Massard da Fonseca, E., & Peralta-Santos, A. (2021). *Coronavirus politics: The comparative politics and policy of COVID-19*. University of Michigan Press.

Hankinson, R. J. (2003). Philosophy and science. In D. Sedley (Ed.), *The Cambridge Companion to Greek and Roman philosophy* (pp. 271–299). Cambridge University Press.

Hanson, A. E. (1975). Hippocrates: "Diseases of women 1". *Signs: Journal of Women in Culture and Society, 1*(2), 567–584.

Harden, V. A. (2009). *WWI and the Ransdell Act of 1930. A short history of the National Institutes of Health*, Office of History National Institutes of Health.

Henning, D. H. (2002). *A Manual for Buddhism and Deep Ecology (Special Edition)*. Bangkok: The World Buddhist University.

Hollingshead, A. B. (1973). Medical Sociology: A Brief Review. The Milbank Memorial Fund Quarterly. *Health and Society*, 51(4), 531–542.

Holman, H. R. (1976). The 'excellence' deception in medicine. *Hospital Practice, 11*(4), 11–21.

Huchzermeyer, W., & Zimmermann, J. (2002). *The Bhagavad Gita as a Living Experience*. Lantern Books.

Illich, I. (1971). *Deschooling society*. Harper & Row.

Illich, I. (1973). *Tools of conviviality*. Harper & Row.

Ilhch, I. (1975). *Medical nemesis*. Colombia University Press.

Illich, I. (1978). *The Right to Useful Unemployment*. New York: Marion Boyars.

Illich, I. (1990). *Health as one's own responsibility: no, thank you!*, Based on a speech given in Hannover, Germany, September 14, 1990 (J. Mason, Trans., H. Lee, ed.). https://geffle.se/illich_archive/1990_health_responsibility.PDF. Retrieved on December 21, 2023.

James, P. A., Oparil, S., Carter, B. L., Cushman, W. C., Dennison-Himmelfarb, C., Handler, J., Lackland, D. T., LeFevre, M. L., MacKenzie, T. D., Ogedegbe, O., & Smith, S. C. (2014). 2014 Evidence-based guideline for the management of high blood pressure in adults: Report from the panel members appointed to the Eighth Joint National Committee (JNC 8). *JAMA, 311*(5), 507–520.

Jayawickrama, J. S. (2023). "Those who make an enemy of the earth make an enemy of themselves": Climate change and human activities from a South and Southeast Asian perspective. In D. Madhanagopal & S. Momtaz (Eds.), *Climate change and risk in South and Southeast Asia: Socio-political perspectives* (pp. 19–35). Routledge.

References

Johnson, T. (1985). Consultation-liaison psychiatry: Medicine as patient, marginality as practice. In R. A. Hahn, & A. D. Gaines (Eds.), *Physicians of western medicine: Anthropological approaches to theory and practice*. D. Reidel Publishing Company.

Kinsella, K., & Velkoff, V. A. (2001). *An aging world*. U.S. Government Printing Office.

Krieger, N. (2011). *Epidemiology and the people's health: Theory and context*. Oxford University Press.

Kulinski, J., Ofori, E. K., Visotcky, A., Smith, A., Sparapani, R., & Fleg, J. L. (2022). Effects of music on the cardiovascular system. *Trends in Cardiovascular Medicine, 32*(6), 390–398.

Lenoir, T., & Hays, M. (2000). The Manhattan project for biomedicine. In P. Sloan (Ed.), *Controlling our destinies* (pp. 19–46). University of Notre Dame Press.

Lin, S. G. (1995). Geopolitics of communicable diseases: Plague in Surat, 1994. *Economic and Political Weekly, 30*(46), 2912–2914.

Lock, M. M., & Nguyen, V. K. (2018). *An anthropology of biomedicine*. John Wiley & Sons.

Löwy, I. (2011). Historiography of biomedicine: "Bio," "medicine," and in between. *Isis, 102*(1), 116–122.

Machan, T. R. (1986). The virtue of freedom in capitalism. *Journal of Applied Philosophy, 3*(1), 49–58.

Mackenbach, J. P. (2009). Politics is nothing but medicine at a larger scale: Reflections on public health's biggest idea. *Journal of Epidemiology & Community Health, 63*(3), 181–184.

Maestri, N. (2020). Diego de Landa (1524–1579), Bishop and inquisitor of early colonial Yucatan. https://www.thoughtco.com/diego-de-landa-inquisitor-colonial-yucatan-171622. Retrieved on October 02, 2023.

Malamitsi-Puchner, A. (2021). Recommendations of Ancient Greek and Byzantine physicians and philosophers on perinatal nutrition and care. *Acta Paediatrica, 110*(8), 2344–2347.

Mariam-Webster Dictionary. (2023). *Normal*. https://www.merriam-webster.com/dictionary/normal. Retrieved on December 05, 2023.

Mignolo, W. D. (2009). Epistemic disobedience, independent thought and decolonial freedom. *Theory, Culture & Society, 26*(7–8), 159–181.

Mignolo, W. D. (2012). *Local histories-global designs: Coloniality, subaltern knowledges, and border thinking*. Princeton University Press.

Nelson, E. S. (2011). The Yijing and philosophy: From Leibniz to Derrida. *Journal of Chinese Philosophy, 38*(3), 377–396.

Ngomane, M. (2019). *Everyday Ubuntu*. Transworld Publishers.

O'Connor, G. T., Neas, L., Vaughn, B., Kattan, M., Mitchell, H., Crain, E. F., Evans, R., 3rd., Gruchalla, R., Morgan, W., Stout, J., Adams, G. K., & Lippmann, M. (2008). Acute respiratory health effects of air pollution on children with asthma in US inner cities. *The Journal of Allergy and Clinical Immunology, 121*(5), 1133-1139.e1.

O'Keefe, P. (2020). Production of nature re-visited. Antipode Online. https://antipodeonline.org/wp-content/uploads/2020/07/OKeefe-2020_Production-of-Nature-Re-Visited_Antipode-Online.pdf. Retrieved on October 20, 2023.

Pescosolido, B. A., & Kronenfeld, J. J. (1995). Health, Illness, and Healing in an Uncertain Era: Challenges from and for medical sociology. *Journal of Health and Social Behavior*, 5–33.

Podur, J. (2022). Talking to Vijay Prashad about "Modernization". *Countercurrents*. https://countercurrents.org/2022/01/talking-to-vijay-prashad-about-modernization/. Retrieved on November 24, 2023.

Ramacharaka, Y. (1904). *Hatha yoga*. Yogi Publication Society.

Rodney, W. (1972). *How Europe underdeveloped Africa?* Pambazuka Press.

Sabahelzain, M. M., Hartigan-Go, K., & Larson, H. J. (2021). The politics of COVID-19 vaccine confidence. *Current Opinion in Immunology, 71*, 92–96.

Satchidananda, S. (2012). *The Yoga Sutras of Patanjali*. Integral Yoga Publications.

Sedley, D. (Ed.). (2003). *The Cambridge companion to Greek and Roman philosophy*. Cambridge University Press.

Sell, S. K., & Williams, O. D. (2020). Health under capitalism: A global political economy of structural pathogenesis. *Review of International Political Economy, 27*(1), 1–25.

Sen, A. (1999). *Development as freedom*. Random House.

Shiloah, A. (1995). *Music in the world of Islam: A socio-cultural study*. Wayne State University Press.

Shiloah, A. (2007). Jewish and Muslim traditions of music therapy. In P. Horden (Ed.), *Music as medicine* (pp. 69–83). Routledge.

Silvano, G. (2021). A brief history of Western medicine. *Journal of Traditional Chinese Medical Sciences, 8*, S10–S16.

Sivaramakrishnan, K. (2011). The return of epidemics and the politics of global–Local health. *The American Journal of Public Health, 101*(6), 1032–1041.

Smith, A. (1776). *An inquiry into the nature and causes of the wealth of nations*. W. Strahan and T. Cadell.

Smith, N. (2000). Afterword: Who rules this sausage factory? *Antipode, 32*(3), 330–339.

Smith, N., & O'Keefe, P. (1980). Geography, Marx, and the concept of nature. *Antipode, 12*(2), 30–39.

Sorrell, R. D. (2009) *St. Francis of Assisi and nature: Tradition and innovation in Western Christian attitudes toward the environment* (2009; online edn, Oxford Academic, 3 Oct. 2011). https://doi.org/10.1093/acprof:oso/9780195386738.001.0001. Retrieved on April 16, 2024.

Staal, F. (2008). *Discovering the Vedas: Origins, mantras, rituals, insights*. Penguin Books.

Starfield, B. (2000). Is US health really the best in the world? *Jama, 284*(4), 483–485.

Taylor, R., & Rieger, A. (1985). Medicine as social science: Rudolf Virchow on the typhus epidemic in Upper Silesia. *International Journal of Health Services, 15*(4), 547–559.

Tharoor, S. (2016). *An era of darkness: The British empire in India*. Aleph.

Tinetti, M. E., & Fried, T. (2004). The end of the disease era. *The American Journal of Medicine, 116*(3), 179–185.

Tountas, Y. (2009). The historical origins of the basic concepts of health promotion and education: The role of ancient Greek philosophy and medicine. *Health Promotion International, 24*(2), 185–192.

Valles, S. (2020). Philosophy of Biomedicine. In E. N. Zalta (Ed.), *The Stanford encyclopedia of philosophy* (Summer 2020 edition). Metaphysics Research Lab, Stanford University. https://plato.stanford.edu/archives/sum2020/entries/biomedicine/. Retrieved on November 02, 2023.

Van Wietmarschen, H. A., Wortelboer, H. M., & van der Greef, J. (2018). Grip on health: A complex systems approach to transform health care. *Journal of Evaluation in Clinical Practice, 24*(1), 269–277.

Vaughan, M. (1991). *Curing their Ills: Colonial power and african illness*. Stanford University Press.

Virchow, R. (1848). *Mittheilungen über die in Oberschlesien herrschende Typhus-Epidemie*. G. Reimer.

Virchow, R. C. (2006). Report on the typhus epidemic in Upper Silesia. *American Journal of Public Health, 96*(12), 2102–2105.

Waitzkin, H. (2020). Moving beyond capitalism for our health. *International Journal of Health Services, Planning, Administration, Evaluation, 50*(4), 458–462.

Wignaraja, P. (1991). *Participatory development: Learning from South Asia*. United Nations University Press.

Willich, S. N., & Berghöfer, A. (2013). George Wolff (1886–1952): Spreading the legacy of Alfred Grotjahn to the United States. *American Journal of Public Health, 103*(12), 2202–2203.

Wittgenstein, L. (1921). *Tractatus Logico-Philosophicus*. Kegan Paul.

Woodwell, D. A. (1999). *National ambulatory medical care survey: 1997 summary*. National Center for Health Statistics; Advance Data from Vital and Health Statistics, No. 305.

World Health Organization. (1948). *Constitution of the World Health Organization*. https://apps.who.int/gb/bd/PDF/bd47/EN/constitution-en.pdf?ua=1. Retrieved on October 20, 2023.

Zelinsky, W. (1975). The Demigod's dilemma. *Annals of the Association of American Geographers, 65*(2), 123–142.

Chapter 3
Defining Health and Wellbeing Through Ancient South Asian Philosophies

3.1 The Health Complexities of South Asia

> Further predictions in the dynamic human body never could prove correct. Doctors have been predicting the unpredictable for decades. The story repeats in the area of cancer and AIDS. While cancer has not been defeated even with all our publicity, a recent world congress of AIDS showed that all the expensive new drugs did not change either the mortality or morbidity scenario.
>
> Hegde (2015, p. 190)

Despite its glorious cultural heritage and native medicinal systems, in the contemporary period, South Asia is also infamously known for its low life expectancy and high rates of malnutrition, infant mortality, lifestyle diseases, and the excessive prevalence of TB and HIV/AIDS, which can also be compared with sub-Saharan Africa, one of the poorest and underdeveloped regions of the world (World Bank, 2023). The rapid population growth, ethnic, religious, and caste-based inequalities, governance complications, and other socioeconomic inequalities in South Asia have already resulted in major health and wellbeing challenges for billions of South Asia. These challenges include poor sanitation, poor maternal health, poor access to healthcare services, widespread malaria, and an emerging epidemic of chronic diseases. Over the past few decades, South Asia has seen both a dramatic rise in various cardiovascular diseases and as well as an increase in longevity, which is contradictory. As identified by CRED (2023), natural hazards such as floods, droughts, and landslides have rapidly risen in South Asia, and they are most likely to increase more in the future. IPCC continues to warn about the projected impacts of climate change, including flooding, heatwaves, drought-related conditions, air pollutants, and its direct and indirect effects on the rise of mental disorders, vector-borne diseases, and several other allergic conditions (Shaw et al., 2022). The interplay and nexus among poverty, disasters, and societal and political conflicts have created major obstacles to the health and wellbeing of South Asians, which will likely intensify in the future. Of course, other regions of the world indeed grapple with these complications. However, we

© The Author(s), under exclusive license to Springer Nature Singapore Pte Ltd. 2025
J. Jayawickrama and D. Madhanagopal, *Reintroducing Nature into Health and Wellbeing*, https://doi.org/10.1007/978-981-96-3090-5_3

underline that the regions once renowned for their cultural superiority, indigenous medicinal systems, and healing practices are now mostly known for all the social, environmental, political, and health risks.

Nevertheless, in an optimistic sense, we hope that these challenges provide certain opportunities for us to employ or at least acknowledge the native medical systems and generational beliefs of South Asians and revisit our conventional understandings to counter the ongoing and future health and wellbeing crises. For South Asians, their historical engagement with nature and traditional knowledge systems (including medicine) can be leveraged and utilized to cope with the sufferings they face in the contemporary period and future challenges. This chapter is one such attempt to get learnings from their historical experiences.

While acknowledging the ancient medical systems in all the South Asian countries—Afghanistan, Bangladesh, Bhutan, India, Maldives, Nepal, Sri Lanka, and Pakistan, this chapter takes Ayurveda and Siddha as two prominent examples to define health and wellbeing beyond the biomedical definitions. To begin, we briefly provide a succinct overview of the health complexities of South Asia through a critical perspective. Then, we take Ayurveda and Siddha as two examples to elaborate on the history and approaches to health and wellbeing. Here, we discuss the critique of the traditional medical systems within biomedicine, especially from a colonial perspective. By presenting the agitation of the Indian Medical Association towards traditional medical systems, we indicate it with the colonial legacy. Throughout this chapter, we put forth the readers to consider a different epistemological understanding of traditional medical systems in South Asia, which is located within the natural processes and natural systems. Through this chapter, we bring forward the discussions of traditional medicinal systems and approaches in South Asia, and we argue and highlight the ways in which they are unique and as well as inevitable.

3.1.1 South Asia and the Three Stages of Epidemiological Transition: A Few Questions

As Omran (1998) put forth, there are three stages of epidemiological transition: *Stage 1*, the pre-industrial period, the mortality rates were high due to the predominance of epidemics and famine, referred to as the "Age of Pestilence and Famine." *Stage 2*, "The age of receding Pandemics," was when epidemics receded, and famines seemed to decline. This was the period where population growth was sustained and began to increase. *Stage 3*, "The Age of Degenerative and [Hu]man-Made Diseases," refers to the period of the past few decades where mortality rates and as well as fertility rates of the countries continued to decrease. The average life expectancy of the countries has gradually exceeded more than 50 years. This age of degenerative and human-made diseases began mainly after 1945; this phase has become more distinct since World War II. The predominance of human-made diseases and the deaths related to lifestyle changes have become more distinct in almost all Western nations, which was highly apparent in the case of Japan. It has become more distinct in developing nations since the 1970s. Since 1970s, we argue that a sea-change in lifestyle and a continuous rise of cardiovascular and malignant related diseases have been witnessed in the developing world, particularly in the South Asian countries over the past four decades.

We also bring forth the limitations of the three epidemiological transition stages, as suggested by Vicziany (2021). Vicziany (2021) argues that the distinctions among these three stages are not evident and are blurred due to the overlapping and interrelated nature of these diseases. She further brings recent research reports on Asthma in India, noting that around 6% and 2% of children and adults in India suffer from Asthma, which is a chronic inflammatory-autoimmune condition. A large proportion of the Indian population tends to hide this disease due to embarrassment and social stigma, which leads to un- and underdiagnosed and largely untreated. She also highlights the ways in which the Indian government prioritizes certain diseases as lifestyle diseases, and the links between mental health and individuals' susceptibility to infectious, non-infectious, and autoimmune diseases further complicate the distinctions between these diseases. Overall, all these complications and the blurriness challenge the rigid categorization and oversimplification of the three stages of epidemiological transition (Vicziany, 2021).

The trends of the rise of life expectancy since the 1950s have been similar in the case of Southeast Asian countries as well. However, some countries, such as Myanmar and Cambodia, have shown limited progress compared to the other Southeast countries due to their history of political conflicts. Many socialist states of Southeast countries reformed their health systems in the 1990s, and thereby, market economies and the global markets have slowly occupied their health systems. Private entities have already started playing indispensable roles in the health systems of many Southeast nations (Chongsuvivatwong et al., 2011). In some countries, hybrid forms of health systems are a combination of public and private entities and are highly subsidized by the state (Barraclough, 2000; Phua, 1991). In this context, it is essential to highlight that Southeast Asia is one of the major hubs where traditional health practices are still vibrant, along with the utilization of biomedical approaches and medical technologies (Chongsuvivatwong et al., 2011).

3.2 Traditional South Asian Medical Systems

We live in a world where everything we do is measured in various quantities. The food we eat, water we drink, steps we walk, income and expenditure, health, wellbeing, and happiness are all measured. In Chap. 2, we argued that this measurement-based and quantitative dimension of life does not bring holistic health and wellbeing to individuals or societies. Our engagement with nature and natural processes, relationships, and surroundings are not necessarily included in the biomedical ideas of health and wellbeing. The conceptual foundations of South Asian traditional medical systems are intertwined with philosophical, religious, medical, and spiritual knowledge that emerged more than 5000 years ago in the region. The long history of health and wellbeing traditions originated from the shared wisdoms, values, lived experiences, and cultural practices of South Asians. Gurus, healers, and traditional medical practitioners were integral to alleviating physical, mental, social, and spiritual problems in various South Asian communities. Although biomedical approaches have become the dominant medical system of causality and treatment of illness and diseases in the region, certain traditional medical practices remain intact in many everyday lives in South Asia even today.

South Asian medical knowledge and practices, including Yoga, meditation, Ayurveda, Siddha, Unani, Homoeopathy, and various herbal medicines, have become globally popular and are used in different parts of the contemporary world (Sujatha, 2020). However, we argue that the philosophical foundations of these traditional medical systems in South Asia are poorly understood. The capitalist marketplace uses these South Asian traditional medical practices in part to improve the "efficiency" of individuals. For example, many advertisements in the UK and USA on mindfulness meditation are promoted as a way to improve one's efficiency at the workplace. Mindfulness meditation is to remove oneself from greed, competition, and arrogance—but this is not the case of these advertisements. In this context, this chapter (see Table 3.1)[1] briefly examines the history and philosophical foundations of South Asian medical systems.

The traditional folk medical systems of Afghanistan have been destroyed over many years of war, conflicts, and disasters. However, in many rural regions, people turn to traditional folk medicine. Muslim clergy performs various rituals such as "dam" to blow the breath of healing while reciting prayers. They also write "ta'wiz," healing prayers on paper, to be consumed in water or sewn into the cloth and worn around the patient's neck. Although there is a dearth of research and understanding, the Afghans continue to largely consume herbal and homoeopathic medicine as a part of their lifestyle. Many older people, especially women, possess strong knowledge of various plant-based herbs for various ailments and know when to use them. In our[2] limited engagement with Afghan populations, we observed that these understandings of herbs go beyond the belief systems of Islam. As Hindu and Buddhist philosophies before Islam had influenced Afghanistan, the communities seem to have specific inspirations related to healing, nature, and natural processes. Most women in rural Afghanistan still make pilgrimages to the shrines of certain saints for healing and fertility, which is an example of the influences of Hindu and Buddhist philosophies.

The traditional medical practices in Bangladesh include Ayurveda, Unani, and Homoeopathy[3] as well as herbal medicine, cultural practices, and religious rites. According to Rahmatullah and Biswas (2012), there is considerable knowledge,

---

[1] We emphasize here that this section does not establish a complete picture of South Asian traditional medical systems from a historical or philosophical perspective; however, it points towards the foundational philosophical aspects of these practices.

[2] Here, we indicate the first author of this book, Janaka Jayawickrama.

[3] Founded by the German physician Samuel Hahnemann in 1796. Homeopathy arrived in the Indian sub-continent in early 1800 through travellers, missionaries, and military personnel from Europe.

3.2 Traditional South Asian Medical Systems

Table 3.1 Brief explanation to traditional medical systems in South Asian countries

No	Country	Traditional medical system(s)	Philosophical understanding
01	Afghanistan	Traditional folk medicine	Illnesses are believed to fall into three categories: (i). Illnesses caused by the evil eye or by jendA (evil spirits or "jinn"); (ii). Illnesses caused by an imbalance of fluids or excess of heat and cold in the body; and (iii). Other illnesses, including those known to be contagious and therefore "unavoidable"
02	Bangladesh	Ayurveda, Unani, and Homoeopathy	Based on traditional uses of plants, animals or their products, other natural substances (including some inorganic chemicals), religious verses, cultural practices, and physical manipulations
03	Bhutan	Bhutanese traditional medicine Sowa Rigpa (the science of healing)	Based on Buddhist philosophical teachings
04	India	Ayurveda, Yoga and Naturopathy, Unani, Siddha and Sowa Rigpa, and Homoeopathy (AYUSH)	Based on Hindu, Buddhist, and Jain philosophical teachings. There are certain early European and Islamic influences into these systems too
05	Nepal	Ayurveda, Unani, Homoeopathy, Naturopathy, Amchi, and Acupuncture	Based on Hindu, Buddhist, and various traditional teachings
06	Maldives	Dhivehi Beys (or Dweep Unani)	Based on natural and herbal medical practices
07	Sri Lanka	Ayurveda, Siddha, and Unani medical systems are practised, along with Sri Lankan indigenous traditional medicine (Deshiya Chikitsa)	Based on Buddhist, Hindu, and natural practices of healing
08	Pakistan	Tibb-e-Unani (Greco-Arabic) and Homoeopathy	Based on balancing nature and natural processes

Sources Ahmad et al., (2021), World Health Organization (2020), Rahmatullah and Biswas (2012), Hussain et al., (2012), Gewali and Awale (2008), McKay and Wangchuk (2005), Patwardhan et al., (2015), Borins (1987)

especially about herbal plants, natural systems, and processes among traditional medical practitioners in the country. In rural and urban Bangladesh, people continue to use traditional medicine in parallel with biomedicine. This is similar in the case of many states in India. According to Haque et al. (2018) and Rahman and Hossen (2017), traditional medicine and approaches need further research in Bangladesh and incorporation into the national healthcare system in a systematic way.

In Bhutan, the traditional medical system is called Sowa Rigpa, or the science of healing. This is very much a living tradition, and in the recent past, Sowa Rigpa has been integrated into the public health structures of Bhutan. State health services provide patients with the choice between biomedical or traditional treatment, usually in the same hospital. According to McKay and Wangchuck (2005), much of the Sowa Rigpa approaches in Bhutan are influenced by Buddhist philosophical foundations, especially from Tibet. Some of these teachings can be found in tests known as Gyu shi (four medical tantras). These are considered Tibetan translations of the original texts in Sanskrit (McKay and Wangchuk, 2005).

The traditional medicinal systems of India have a rich history with diverse pathways—Ayurveda, Yoga and Naturopathy, Unani, Siddha and Sowa Rigpa, and Homoeopathy are of the known native medicinal systems. Hindu, Buddhist, and Jain philosophies mainly influence these practices. According to Patwardhan et al. (2015), the Indian medical system is inseparable from the darśanas, or schools of Indian philosophy. However, the Unani pathway of medicine has the foundations laid by Hippocrates (460 BC) and later by Galen (Roman and Greek physician, surgeon, and philosopher, 129–216 AD). They developed this medical approach based on observation and experiment with a method of taking patients' medical histories (Borins, 1987). Naturopathy in India has been strongly connected to Yoga, which promotes natural cure for ailments.[4] All these explanations are not to assert that these medicinal systems are exclusively native, unique, and indigenous. Instead, we also highlight that the Indian philosophies combined with specific external influences, have influenced nearly all the above-said medicinal systems in South Asia.

Nepal's traditional medical system combines Ayurveda, Unani, Homoeopathy, Naturopathy, Amchi, and Acupuncture. Two different paths are being adopted in Nepal for health delivery. First, medical providers, and second, faith healers. In this, we focus on medical providers based on medical pathways. The Nepali traditional medical system is mainly influenced by Hindu and Buddhist philosophies. Although the practices of Unani and Acupuncture are not based on these philosophical influences, the practices can be understood within Hindu and Buddhist frameworks. According to Gewali and Awale (2008), the herbal and plant-based aspects of the traditional medical system in Nepal have been popular among the population who seek treatments for various ailments.

For centuries, Maldivians traditionally rely on their native medicinal systems for health and wellbeing. Maldivian traditional medicine has been influenced by India, Malaysia, Sri Lanka, China, and Arab and Persian travellers. Over the centuries, this acquired knowledge has been synthesized and developed into local herbal remedies, which can be identified as Dhivehi Beys. Besides our limited engagement with the people of Maldives, finding research on the traditional medical system has been arduous.

Heavily influenced by Indian traditional medicine, Ayurveda, Siddha, and Unani are popular within the Sri Lankan traditional medical system. Along with this, the indigenous medical practices called Deshiya Chikitsa are equally popular in Sri

---

[4] A form of alternative medicine with roots in the 19th-century "natural cure" movement in Europe.

Lanka. Hindu and Buddhist philosophies continue to influence the most health frameworks of Sri Lanka. According to Weragoda (1980), Ayurveda and Deshiya Chikitsa mainly use plants and herbal preparations to treat illnesses and diseases.

The two main pathways of the traditional medical system in Pakistan are Tibb-e-Unani and Homoeopathy. Both these pathways are outside the Indian sub-continent. However, there is a strong focus on nature and natural processes. The fundamentals of Tibb-e-Unani, which is the Greco-Arabic approach, the human body is made up of the four basic elements of water, air, earth, and fire with different temperaments such as cold, hot, wet, and dry (Hussain et al., 2012). The homoeopathic medical pathway was introduced to the South Asian subcontinent a little over a century ago and has blended with the traditional concepts of healing in Pakistan. According to Hussain et al. (2012), Homoeopathy is based on the natural law of healing, which means healing the like. Both these approaches have strong connections to nature and natural processes of health and wellbeing.

In short, most native medicinal systems of South Asia have historically been influenced by Hindu and Buddhist philosophies, which connect to nature and natural processes. Even the non-native medical pathways such as Unani and Homoeopathy interacted and integrated with local herbal medical practices of South Asia which again connect with natural processes such as seasons and circadian rhythm. According to the World Health Organization (2020), traditional medical systems are based on a blend of spiritual and empirical sources based on generational knowledge of lived experiences. The then Director-General of WHO, Dr. Margaret Chan, 2014 firmly acknowledged the contribution of Traditional and Complementary Medicine (T&CM) to improve the health and wellbeing of populations and the comprehensiveness of most traditional medical systems and healthcare (World Health Organization, 2020).

3.3 Defining Health and Wellbeing from Ancient Wisdoms: Ayurveda and Siddha

As explained in the previous section, historically, South Asia possesses a rich history of traditional medicinal systems, and in most cases, they have been integrated with the philosophies, religions, and customs of the region. Ayurveda, the science of life, is one of the rich ancient medicinal systems of ancient India; it deals not only with diseases but also the prevention of illnesses, the smooth functioning of the human body in constitution with nature, and provides a profound understanding of the human's way of life, health and the idea of holistic health and balanced life in align with nature. In recent decades, the knowledge production on the history, principles, values, approaches, and contributions of Ayurveda has been extensive (Jaiswal & Williams, 2017; Narayanaswamy, 1981). Here, we selectively chose some noteworthy works, and based on that, we provide a few insights into how health and wellbeing can be understood and interpreted in the contemporary period.

Ayurveda

Ayurveda, one of the renowned medicinal systems in ancient India, dates back to the second century BC (Jaiswal & Williams, 2017). Wujastyk (2003) explains that the roots of Ayurveda lie in Vedic literature. Ayurveda evolved as a distinct medicinal system from Vedic literature some two thousand years ago, with the three prominent and influential Medical Compendiums, Charaka, Susruta, and Bhela, serving as a foundation of ancient Indian medicinal systems. The origins and history of Ayurveda have been controversial, and we still do not have strong and consistent evidence regarding the period of its origin. Nevertheless, scholars widely agree that Ayurveda evolved with the development of ancient Indian philosophical and religious traditions. Among traditional Ayurvedic scholars, there is a belief that the creator of the Universe, Brahma, evolved the science of Ayurveda and taught this to Prajapati Daksha. And it believed that the Ayurvedic knowledge was passed over to Asvins and Indra, which in turn passed over to the Sages of the ancient period, and from them, the knowledge was passed to classical Susruta and Charaka tradition, and from them, it was passed over to their disciples, and then to the general public through various slokas, writings, and oral narrations.[5] Ayurveda is also believed to have originated in the Vedic period (5000–1000 BCE), roughly 3000 to 7000 years ago, as even the oldest Vedas have references to various medicinal plants and natural resources for the treatment of illnesses (Jaiswal & Williams, 2017; Larson, 1987; Mukherjee et al., 2017). Another Sanskrit practitioner for decades, Swami Sadashiva Tirtha, writes that Sanskrit is the world's first medicine, which is 5000 years old. As he argues, before the development/arrival of Ayurveda, the world used to have healers—early humans used to depend on medicinal plants and herbs to cure illnesses. Compared to those ancient healing techniques, Ayurveda was one of the most comprehensive, systematic, and holistic medicines available of the ancient period (Tirtha, 2005). Pollock (1989) clarified the discrepancies, absence, and problem of the history of texts in ancient India, and he links it with the Mimamsa tradition, a Brahminical discipline that denied the relevance of history in the pursuit of knowledge and discouraged referentiality, which resulted in most Sanskrit texts we get no references relating to Authors' names and years.

> As he writes: "…To an astonishing degree Sanskrit texts are anonymous or pseudonymous, or might just as well be. The strategy of eliminating from the text—whatever sort of text it might be—the personality of the author and anything else that could help us situate the text in time is a formal correlate of a content invariably marked by a historicality. Works on statecraft, for example, describe their subject without specific reference to a single historically existing state…." (Pollock, 1989. p. 606)

Charaka Samhita points towards Dhamma (principles of life), Kama (desires), and Moksha (liberation) are important factors for health and wellbeing (See: Samhita,

---

[5] It is important to note that different researchers of India explain this story in different versions. However, the general belief among Ayurvedic practitioners that Ayurvedic knowledge originally evolved from Brahman remains similar, and most researchers on India widely share it, but the later stages that we noted here may differ. Hence, here, we provide the refined and mostly shared narratives among Indian and Ayurvedic scholars.

1949). This is because the physical, mental, and social components are inherently connected to the spiritual component of health and wellbeing. One does not have to be religious to understand this spiritual component of health and wellbeing. Managing desires—not being greedy and arrogant as well as exclusive by establishing sound principles of life that do not harm oneself or others could facilitate physical, mental, and social health and wellbeing.

The other traditional medicinal systems of those ancient periods conventionally developed their conceptual/philosophical framework based on the results derived from the treatment made by herbs/medical plants/other healing techniques. Ayurveda is fundamentally different from these other ancient medicinal systems as it first developed its philosophical framework and then determined and developed its therapeutic effects. The foundations of Ayurveda primarily lay in the ancient Indian philosophical schools such as Samkhya and Vaisheshika, and it also derives from Vedanta, Nyaya, Yoga, Buddhist, and Jainist systems to a lesser degree. Nyaya, Samkhya, and Vaisheshika schools provide extensive discussions and insights about medicine. In short, Vaisheshika school emphasizes the diagnosis and asks the physician to infer about the patient's health condition before getting treated. The Nyaya school advocates for doctors to know more about the patients' condition and illnesses before proceeding with treatment (Crawford, 2001; Jaiswal & Williams, 2017). Here, we also want to highlight the influential book "Science and Society in Ancient India" by Chattopadhyaya (1978), who provided a rational picture of ancient Indian medicine. He argued that early medical Sanskrit texts and physicians transformed from magico-religious therapeutics to non-religious, rational, and secular, and they discarded scripture orientation and provided more importance to reason, observation, and empiricism. In the later era, it underwent a severe process of Hinduization for the sake of the Brahmin elite of the ancient society, too. He also provided strong arguments for the contradictory statements of ancient Sanskrit medicinal texts regarding cow, cow's flesh, and sex. On the one hand, Sanskrit texts praised cows, highly recommended the worship of cows, and argued that cows are the holy objects of the gods and the Brahmins. On the other hand, it also recommends the utilization of cow's flesh to treat illnesses such as fever and cough. A similar dual attitude also goes with the case of sex and alcohol.

In the words of Chattopadhyaya:

"Indian medicine takes the step from magico-religious therapeutics to rational therapeutics sometime before the Buddha." (Chattopadhyaya, 1978, p. 341)

……But this emphasis of the importance of empirical data in Ayurveda must not be misunderstood. It means no doubt that according to the ancient doctors, their science is impossible without depending on empirical data or that the stock of empirical data ultimately differentiates science from the empty postulates of pure reason………….. Still the point is that all these never allow them to forget the basic fact that empirical knowledge forms the ultimate foundation of their science.[6] One of the strongest points of Ayurveda is the accumulation of an enormous amount of empirical data on which are based its theoretical generalisations. (Chattopadhyaya, 1978, p. 84)

---

[6] Ayurveda: Particularly, Chattopadhyaya notes about Charaka Samhita here.

As noted earlier, several reviews and works discuss the detailed history of Ayurveda and its approaches. For example, Tirtha (2005, 3–9) provides a detailed but concise description of the origin of Ayurveda, eight branches of Ayurveda, its approaches, and also the decline of Ayurveda. Like this, Vasant Lad, another renowned scholar and practitioner of Ayurveda, provides a detailed outline of the history and philosophy of Ayurveda (Lad, 2002). Over the centuries, Sanskrit nurtured and evolved into two primary schools—Dhanvantri Sampradaya (School of Physicians) and Atreya Sampradaya (School of Surgeons), and eight different specializations. These schools of physicians and surgeons have their representative compilations, known as (i) Charaka Samhita: contains a detailed list of various aspects of medicine, medicinal plants, herbs, and minerals (with their origins) used for treating illnesses, and (ii) Susruta Samhita: believed to have been written by Susruta, the father of plastic surgery in India. Though we do not have concrete evidence on the birth and history of Susruta, we have many speculations about Susruta and his Samhita. He was believed to have been born in Bihar, currently in eastern India, and was the first to practice rhinoplasty in India. Susruta means "that which is well heard" or one who has thoroughly learned by hearing. Through Vedic hymns, we can also speculate that he might have lived around 1000 BCE.[7] Susruta Samhita details surgical matters, including how to perform the surgery, and more than 100 surgical instruments are described, including scalpels, scissors, and more. Along with the descriptions of various anatomical procedures to be followed during surgery. Susruta Samhita also describes around 600 drugs and discusses other surgery-related topics (Chari, 2003; Loukas et al., 2010; Ravishankar & Shukla, 2007).

Most importantly, Ayurveda lists the code of conduct and principles that Vaidyans (physicians/doctors) should follow, which brings further questions that whether these age-old ethics are continued to be followed by the Ayurvedic physicians of the contemporary world—if not, it also raises concerns on the ways in which it can influence or integrate with the Western biomedicine. Ayurveda postulates several codes for an individual to lead a healthy, balanced, and happy life. They are Dinacharya (rules for daily regimen), Ratricharya (rules for night regimen), Ritucharya (routine that can be maintained seasonally), and Sadvritta (code of good conduct for mental health and social behaviour). Importantly, Sadvritta can be applied to all individuals throughout the year irrespective of the places and backgrounds that they belong to. These codes play critical roles in clearing all the important channels of the human body, resulting in the efficient functioning and comfort to brain (Himanshu et al., 2002).

Siddha

The other traditional medical pathway that this chapter focuses on is Siddha. Like Ayurveda, Siddha medicine also possesses a rich history. Siddha has a strong

---

[7] It is important to highlight that we do not have any strong and consistent views among the scholars on the lives and periods of Charaka and Samhita, and so the periods that both Charaka Samhita and Susruta Samhita were written. For example, in the work on the development of Ayurveda, Mukherjee et al. (2017) write that both the Samhitas were written before sixth century CE.

3.3 Defining Health and Wellbeing from Ancient Wisdoms: Ayurveda ...

Dravidian origin and is mostly popular in southern India, Sri Lanka, Malaysia, Singapore, Mauritius, and some of the Southeast Asian countries (Ministry of AYUSH, 2019).

Madhavan (1984, p. 12) defines definition of Siddha as follows:

> The word "Siddha" comes from the word "Siddhi" which means "an object to be attained" or "perfection" or "heavenly bliss." Generally, the Siddhars are considered to be super-human beings who have defined age and other laws of nature to which all human beings are subject to.

White (1997, p. 2) defines the word Siddha as follows:

> As a common noun, Siddha means "realized, perfected one," a term generally applied to a practitioner {*sädhaka, sädhit*) who has through his practice {*sädhana*) realized his dual goal of superhuman powers (siddhis, "realizations," "perfections") and bodily immortality (*Jivamukti*).

Weiss (2009) emphasizes, the legacy and popularity of Siddha Vaidyas in Tamil Nadu today go back to the contribution of Tamil revivalist writers of the early twentieth century who portrayed them as egalitarians and scientific, and the Vaidyas who represent the indigenous Tamil science. Even today, many popular Siddha Vaidyas usually relate the origins of their knowledge to a group of Yogis known as Siddhars (perfected individuals).

Continuing this, Madhavan (1984, p. 17–18) posits that humans may achieve eight supernatural/miraculous powers through Yogic practice, as follows. This was propounded by Thirumular, one of the eighteen Siddhars, whose birth and period are controversial and not known. (i) Anima (Flying). (ii) Mahima (Expansion). (iii) Karima (The power to condense the primordial elements within oneself into a chosen point or location). (iv) Lahima (Lightness). (v) Prapthi (Power of knowing everything, including past, present, and the future). (vi) Prahamiyam (The power of penetration like rays so that one can be immortal) (vii) Esathuvam (Supreme power over animates and inanimates). viii. Vasithuvam (Power to secure anything). White (1997, p. 57) clarifies that,

> Siddha provides different meanings in the contemporary Indian landscape. Since the Gupta period in ancient India (4th – 6th Century), in both Hindu and Buddhist schools, different sects and traditions have been identified with this term in different interpretations. He writes, "The original referent of the term was a class of demigods: in Buddhist and Hindu traditions alike, the Siddhas shared the interface between earth and sky—mountain tops and the atmospheric region—with a horde (gana) of semidivine beings.

In Tamil Nadu today, Siddha is mainly associated with Vaidyas or Vaidyar (meaning physician) (Weiss, 2009; White, 1997). One of the famous books on Siddha medicine published in Tamil Nadu by the International Institute of Tamil Nadu Studies, administered by the state government of Tamil Nadu, is Siddha Medical Manuscripts in Tamil (Editor: Madhavan, 1984). This book traces the roots of Siddhars and Siddha medicine to a very ancient period, however, accepts that the history of Siddhars has yet to be written. Also, as he asserts, the total number of Siddhars might be more than hundreds, though there was a long tradition of referring to them as eighteen. This is because there might have only been available works of eighteen Siddhars during the compilation of their works. Here, Madhavan's reclarification on the total number of Siddhars should also be considered. As he notes, there were only nine Siddhars, and the numbers (groupings) of Siddhars became eighteen, popularly known as "Pathinen Siddhars." From Madhavan's writings, we can infer that the origin and number of Siddhars, including their contributions, are still unknown. Despite this, he claims that the contributions of Siddhars were extraordinary, not just to alchemy and medicine but also to arts, literature, philosophy, religion, spirituality, morality, and the way of life of ancient Tamils (Madhavan, 1984).

Without noting further details of the specific Siddhars and relevant information, Madhavan (1984) further expands the contributions of Siddhars, noting their deep knowledge of alchemy, chemistry, mercury, sulphur, salts, and the preparation of medicines from these metals and elements. However, he also points out Siddhars often used secret herbs and plants relating to medicine, Yoga, and wisdom. They intentionally kept these practices hidden from the public to prevent misuse. According to Madhavan (1984), among the most renowned and ancient Siddhars are Agathiyar and Thirumoolar—both of their time periods are controversial and still uncertain. By analysing Thirumoolar's literary style, he speculates that his period likely falls after the Christian era as Thirumoolar incorporated several words that were of Sanskritic origin. He also highlights that the majority of their writings have been lost over time, and many works attributed to them are, in fact, spurious creations by later plagiarists. Nonetheless, their impact on Siddha medicine, education, and Tamil culture was undeniably significant.

Zimmermann (2001), by quoting the works of Venkatraman (1990) and Thirunarayanan (1993) writes that Siddhars were a class of free thinkers of ancient Tamil society, and their works dealt with alchemy, medicine, culture, philosophy, and other tantric rituals; however, their works were not researched extensively, leading into many misinterpretations of their creations, creators, and the genuineness of the medicines that they propounded. Also, the different linguistic styles of the verses of many Siddhars (available today) are pedestrian, which leads us to speculate that they are actually the forgeries of the later quacks. As Venkatraman (1990) writes, it was sure that some historical Siddhars might belong to the tenth century period. Nevertheless, the famous medicinal contributions of Siddhars that are available today might belong to the sixteenth and eighteenth centuries. This contradicts the views of Thirunarayanan (1993), who argues that almost all the Siddhars belong to the seventh and twelfth centuries, and so do their contributions. Overall, by reviewing the works on Siddhas and Siddha medicine, Zimmermann (2001) finds some of the complications of Siddha medicine, which are as follows:

(i) Siddha medicine remains relatively unexplored and under-researched and largely controversial (mainly on the time periods) even in the contemporary period. Most Siddha writings appear to have been authored after the fifteenth century. However, efforts have been made by Tamil Siddha practitioners to trace its origins back to ancient Tamil civilization and to connect with Tamil pride and Tamil utopia.

(ii) Siddha medicine is fundamentally rooted in spiritualism rather than materialism. Consequently, promoting and marketing medicines based on spiritual principles in today's competitive and materialistic world may pose challenges.
(iii) Despite the controversies between Ayurveda and Siddha, which emerged first, there might be more possibilities for mutual exchanges between these two medicinal systems. Evidence suggests that Siddha alchemy and medicine were once a pan-Indian phenomenon but are now primarily limited to Tamil Nadu and, to a lesser extent, Kerala. Even within Tamil Nadu, Siddha medicine is not widely embraced and remains largely unexplored from a systematic and scientific perspective.

For example, Sébastia (2010) studied the case of two Siddha practitioners of Tamil Nadu and discussed their approach to treating ailments, particularly diabetes. The first case concerns Jeyaram and Neela (Husband and Wife), who practice Siddha medicine by owning a large in-and out-patient clientele based in Kanyakumari district, a southernmost district of Tamil Nadu. This hospital possesses the clinical test room, radiography, and other facilities used in Allopathy medicine to detect and treat the diseases. Although Jeyaram lacks formal accreditation in Siddha medicine, he acquired his medical knowledge from his father and grandfather, who were esteemed Siddha Vaidyas in the region. Additionally, he is skilled in Homoeopathy practice. On the other hand, his wife Neela holds a BSMS degree (Bachelor of Siddha Medicine and Surgery), a recognized qualification for practicing Siddha medicine bestowed by the Government of Tamil Nadu, and she is the legal proprietor of this hospital. Together, they offer patient-specific treatments, such as utilizing Siddha medicines prepared by Jayaram's family, for various conditions, including osteoarthritis, diabetic ulcers, and hemiplegia. They also utilize medicines from Allopathy and Ayurveda to treat their patients to complement their traditional drugs and have their own justifications for doing so. The second case deals with Rattinammal, an 86-year-old Siddha practitioner in Madurai who belongs to the traditional Raja Vaittiyar family (a social group, also considered a caste who used to provide medicinal treatment to Kings and their families in ancient Tamil Nadu) that practices Siddha medicine differently, unlike the first case. She prepares all her medicine with the assistance of her disciple, a retired lawyer keen on learning Siddha medicine for the service of people. Her focus primarily revolves around treating diabetes patients, with most of her clientele from the urban middle class. Many of these diabetes patients seek her out in critical situations, fearing the need for organ amputation. Rattinammal developed her diabetes treatment formulations, including "cakkarai cūranam," about two decades ago by studying plant-based remedies mentioned in Siddha texts and consulting various sources. Her treatments have been successful, supported by patient outcomes. Importantly, Rattinammal considers the psychological wellbeing of her patients and incorporates non-conventional methods and her alchemical knowledge into her treatment approach. This differs from Jeyaram, who avoids non-conventional treatments and magic, fearing it may label him quack and unprofessional. By examining these two cases of Siddha practitioners, as an anthropologist, Sébastia (2010) acknowledges their traditional Siddha way of healing knowledge, capacity to understand the disease, adaptability, and flexibility in treatment contribute to successful outcomes in treating patients with diabetic ulcers and osteoarthritis.

In India, according to the Ministry of AYUSH (2019), the Siddha medical approach has strong foundations reflecting the culture, tradition, and heritage of the sub-continent. Further, the Ministry of AYUSH states that the Siddha system has four main divisions:

1. Chemistry/Iatrochemistry alchemy.
2. Treatment.
3. Yogic practices.
4. Wisdom.

This approach of Siddha is based on ninety-six tools, which include physical, physiological, psychological, and intellectual dimensions of every human being. Among the ninety-six tools, the five elements are the fundamental units for every human body and the Cosmos. The Siddhars that are practicing Yoga maintain a highly evolved consciousness, intellect, and institution, which allow them to explore the world around them and utilize its natural resources to improve wellbeing of human beings. The strength of the Siddha medical approach is based on its holistic methodology—the physical, mental, social, and spiritual wellbeing by adapting simple lifestyle practices, dietary regimens, and usage of nature-based drugs.

The following example shows that promoting health and wellbeing is a deep understanding of responsibility towards humanity within Siddha tradition, which is governed by nature and natural processes. The example of Narayana Murty in Shankar et al., (2003, p. 60) explains the commitment to daily rituals and practices, following community rules, service about financial or other forms of benefits, and most importantly considering plants and natural processes as important parts of healing are some of the qualities of a healer. Further, Shankar et al., (2003, p. 60) present that Murty's patients' belief in the good heart and genuine mind of the healer is essential in the healing.

What is essential to understand here is that the medical practitioner is connected to nature and natural processes. Their spiritual practices and engagement with patients have a meaning beyond capital gain. Like in the biomedical approach, there are no pathways for the traditional medical practitioner because they are using their expertise to combine the roles of various specialists into human connections by integrating physical, mental, social, and spiritual health as well as nature during the healing process. The traditional medical practitioner is not a "professional" who expects a financial or material return in providing care for people.[8]

In Ayurveda and Siddha medical approaches, understanding the strong connection between humans and nature is essential. The thought structures of Ayurveda and Siddha, apart from the complicated therapeutics in both approaches, bring a

---

[8] Although, many traditional medical practitioners continue their practices outside to the capital marketplace, we acknowledge that in India, Nepal, and Sri Lanka, the traditional medical practices have been commercialized. In that the biomedicalization of Ayurveda, and Deshiya Chikitsa has become a challenge for traditional medical practitioners that are not "certified" by government institutions or universities.

consistent way of understanding the phenomenal and biological world of humans, plants, and animals through a critical engagement with nature and natural processes. Ayurveda and Siddha bring a more profound recognition of the interrelatedness of body and mind of environment, relationships, food, and medicine. Within the body, there is an explanation based on various physiological processes conceived and described in terms of the five elements—earth, fire, water, air, and ether. The holistic approach is based on the concept of balance, which has the satisfaction of place. The harmony of the body and mind is a precondition for a healthy and purposeful life. The principles of life (dharma), economics and finances (artha), and pleasures of life (kama) of the individual are important to understanding health and wellbeing.

The Ayurvedic explanation or definition of health and wellbeing within this understanding is relevant to contemporary societies. Compared to the WHO definition of health, which requires an expert to certify a healthy individual, the Ayurvedic definition empowers the individual. Sushruta Samhita (sixth century BC) explains that the health and wellbeing of the individual are based on quality sleep and rest, an adequate (not too much or not too little) ratio of food intake to stool output, and a harmonious relationship with society and the environment (Lad, 2002). This is in contrast to the WHO definition of health. From Hindu and Buddhist perspectives, human beings who live in society are supposed to live a meaningful life with complete clarity and concern for all that exists, balancing both material and spiritual lives in parallel (Radhakrishnan, 1950, 1963). According to the Ministry of AYUSH (2019), Siddha's approach to health and wellbeing is similar to the Ayurvedic understanding. Humans are the microcosm of the university, which is the macrocosm. Therefore, the understanding of human beings must come through an understanding of the universe. It is important to understand that microcosm matters are identical to macrocosm matters. Like Ayurveda, the Siddha approach explains the health and wellbeing of the human within nature. Ayurveda and Siddha strongly consider the physical, mental, social, spiritual, and ecological dimensions in facilitating health and wellbeing.

In both traditions of Ayurveda and Siddha, there is an emphasis that the individual human being as a whole is to be examined in detail to understand their health and wellbeing or illnesses and diseases. This is in contrast to the biomedical approach that only focuses on the organ or diseases without considering the whole human being. Even in a patient, their health and wellbeing must be preserved with the cure of the disease.[9] In the Ayurvedic and Siddha traditions, preventative and health promotive approaches are important for healthy human beings. Their daily (dinacharya) and seasonal (rtucharya) routines, food intake, rejuvenating arrangements within their lifestyle, and engagement with nature constitute the preventative and health promotive approaches.

What is important to understand that these philosophical foundations are not just theoretical perspectives, but very much through lived experiences of ancient scientists. Guthrie (1945, p.19) a medical historian explained that,

---

[9] In biomedical approach with cancer treatments, both diseased and healthy cells are destroyed in the process of cure. In that, the individual becomes more vulnerable to future diseases.

"It was in surgery above all that the ancient Hindus excelled. Susruta described more than a hundred instruments. This was their greatest contribution to the art of healing and the work was bold and distinctive. It is not unlikely, though difficult to prove, that some of it was of Greek origin. Some, indeed, state that the Greek drew much of their knowledge from the Hindus."

In that we argue that these ancient traditional medical systems must be taken seriously in improving health and wellbeing of populations.

3.4 Critiques Within: The Case of India

This section presents the challenges between Euro-North American epistemology and South Asian epistemologies. Mignolo (2002, 2009) explains this as the coloniality of knowing, sensing, and thinking. We would call this the colonization of the mind. Since the arrival of European colonizers in the Indian subcontinent in 1505, the native populations were told, pressured, and punished to accept that their knowledge systems were inferior to the European way of knowing. We remind the statement by Macaulay (1835)—the British politician and historian, which pointed that native literature of India are inferior or "useless" compared to European knowledge. What Macaulay suggested to create a class of people that can be a bridge between the colonizers and the colonized.

Since the independence of South Asia, governance, development, health, and education have been following the Euro-North American epistemological foundations. The following account shows the unwillingness or challenges of Euro-North American epistemology to collaborate with South Asian epistemologies related to health and wellbeing.

While tracing Western medicine in Colonial India, Arnold (2000) provides a picture of how Westerners had to acknowledge the existence of well-established therapeutic beliefs and practices in India, and they had to acknowledge the efficacy of traditional medicine systems such as Ayurveda, Unani, and Folk (Country) medicines and their influence over the people of India. The Britishers had less or no interest in the religious aspects of traditional medicinal systems of Vaidyas and Hakims of colonial India; nevertheless, there was a growing recognition of their rich and "useful" knowledge of herbs and medicinal plants, and their efficacy in treating diseases like Cholera and Dysentery, where the Western medicinal systems proved inefficient. Hence, that was a period where Britishers showed interest in translating the remedies of India to English, and that was a period where the interactions between indigenous and Western medicines happened. As Arnold points out, Sir Whitelaw Ainslie, a British Surgeon working for the East India Company, published a book on medicinal plants in India in 1813 entitled "Materia Indica," this book was one of the first attempts to connect medicines between Europe and Asia. Following this, there was a list of continuous translations and publications of Indian medicines and drugs in reputed journals like Transactions of the Medical and Physical Society of Calcutta and text translations such as George Playfair's "Taleef Shereef" in 1833

3.4 Critiques Within: The Case of India

and the Bengal Pharmacopoeia compiled by O'shaughnessy in 1844. All these texts encouraged the exploration of new remedies in India (Arnold, 2000, p. 68).

In this context, Arnold (2000) highlights the financial burden of the colonial government to import the "Peruvian bark" (cinc hona) to treat Malaria. Therefore, the Britishers appreciated the idea of finding local substitutes to treat many diseases, including Malaria, leading to the exploration of new drugs from Indian medicinal systems and botanical investigations. From 1810 to 1830, many efforts were made by British Surgeons such as Benjamin Heyne and Whitelaw Ainslie in Madras and H. H. Wilson in Bengal to study Ayurvedic texts, and J. Forbes Royle, a British Botanist's book entitled "Antiquity of Hindoo Medicine" is one of the seminal efforts of the Britishers to claim the authority of "Hindu medicine." Despite these noted efforts to study and exchange from indigenous Indian medicinal systems, many scepticisms surrounding Ayurveda as it is too mixed with religion, and they shared the opinion that Ayurveda used to be exceptional in ancient times but lost its greatness over the period. Another reason pointed out by those sceptics was that the practice of dissecting bodies, which was mentioned in old Ayurvedic texts, had been forgotten, which made Ayurvedic doctors not very knowledgeable about how the human body works. Another critique of Britishers towards Ayurvedic practitioners of those days was their usage of "dangerous" drugs like arsenic and aconite. However interestingly, they were using aggressive treatments that often did not lead to long-term cures and sometimes even caused more harm; however, western medicine moved away from using such harmful treatments by the mid of the nineteenth century. Overall, Western medicine practitioners' initial interest in Indian traditional medicinal systems spanned around different factors in the early nineteenth century. As time passed, the Western medicine practitioners and the British government felt confident in their knowledge. They started believing they had already learned what they could learn from the ancient Indian texts. They started focusing on European scientific pharmacology and identifying the active chemical components of drugs rather than collecting a wide range of exotic materials noted in Indian traditional medicines, leading to the fading interest in traditional Indian medicine systems. This hampered the efforts and measures of cross-cultural medicinal exchanges at the end of nineteenth-century colonial India (Arnold, 2000, p. 66–69).

> Arnold (1993, pp. 2–3) traces the event in 1908: "As far as the principal of Calcutta's Medical College, C. P. Lukis (soon to be Sir Pardy Lukis and director-general of the IMS), was concerned, the issue brought to prominence by Paltoo's grisly antics in the Burra Bazaar was how such "self-constituted" colleges were to be regulated to ensure that only properly trained and duly qualified doctors and surgeons were given degrees and allowed to practice in India. This revived the old, but increasingly pressing, issue (dating back to the 1880s) of whether there should be a medical registration act for India as there had long been in Britain. Lukis was among those who argued that registration was essential if the standards of Western medicine in India were to be maintained. Bogus degrees issued by unregulated colleges would not only produce poorly qualified doctors and surgeons who would be a danger to their patients and the community among whom they practiced, but they would also by their incompetence and malpractice bring Western medicine as a whole into disrepute...."

The contemporary health and policy systems of India have evolved from one of the landmark reports made in British India amid the Second World War and published in 1946, the "Report on the Health Survey and Development Committee," popularly referred to as the Bhore Committee Report, 1946 (The chairman of this report was Sir Joseph William Bhore). This report provided a broad survey of health systems and organizations in India and recommended future development (Chokshi et al., 2016; Duggal, 1991). When discussing indigenous medicine in India, the Bhore committee (1946, Vol II, p. 455) open with the following statement:

> In considering the question of the place which the indigenous systems of medical treatment should occupy in any planned organization of medical relief and public health in the country, we are faced with certain difficulties. We realize the hold that these systems exercise not merely over the illiterate masses but over considerable sections of the intelligentsia. We have also to recognize that treatment by practitioners of these systems is said to be cheap, and it is claimed that the empirical knowledge, that has been accumulated over centuries has resulted in a fund of experience of the properties and medicinal use of minerals, herbs and plants which is of some value. Further, the undoubted part that these systems have played in the long distant past in influencing the development of medicine and surgery in other countries of the world has naturally engendered a feeling of patriotic pride in the place they will always occupy in any world history of the rise and development of medicine. This feeling has not been without its effect on the value which is attached by some to the practice of these systems.... (Health Survey and Development Committee (Bhore Committee), 1946)

The language of this statement shows the Western bias towards traditional medicine systems of colonial India. For example, the words "Illiterate Masses" versus "Intelligentsia" insinuated that the traditional medicine system is mainly meant for the "illiterate masses." Nevertheless, "intelligentsia" continues to benefit from these medicinal systems. The choice of these words unnecessarily creates a class divide among the people and somehow subtly mentions that it is majorly the choice of the illiterate masses. Also, as pointed out by Wujastyk (2008) in this report, illiterate masses have a "hold" over indigenous medicine. This language makes us think that the illiterate masses of India hold this indigenous medicine in non-rational means, which would typically include the "superstitious" and "unscientific" stuff. Also, this report considers that indigenous medicine is static and unchanging, and it is highly interlinked with "patriotic" and does not have any link with "scientific" and "rational" means that Western medicine holds. Overall, as Wujastyk (2008) clarifies, this Bhore committee clearly undermined the merits of indigenous medicine, sometimes subtly and sometimes openly. It clearly dismissed indigenous medicine without providing any empirical evidence and was not ready to consider the quality of the progress.

Also, this report restricts the affix "doctors" only for the graduates of the Western medicine (Allopathy). One of the Bhore's committee members, R. A. Amesur, then President of the Indian Medical Association (IMA) recommended the following:

(i) no medical practitioner shall be entitled to affix the designation "Doctor" before his name unless he is a registered medical practitioner in modern scientific medicine;
(ii) no person shall be entitled to prescribe drugs which are in, the British Pharmacopoeia, especially injections and poisonous preparations, unless he is a registered medical practitioner; and

3.4 Critiques Within: The Case of India

(iii) those who practice the Unani or Ayurvedic system of medicine may style themselves as "Hakims" or "Vaidyas" as the case may be (Bhore, 1946, Vol II, p. 459).

These three restrictions and the continuing statements of this report (Bhore, 1946, Vol II, p. 459–461) are highly relevant and influential even today, and these restrictions define who "doctors" and who are not. It clearly stipulates that the holder of the Doctor of Medicine is a qualified medical practitioner of scientific medicine, and it also imposes the meaning that any "other" systems of medicine are not scientific and not rational, and it also recommends the right to prescribe particular medicines.

What we observe is the same level of distrust and unwillingness of the biomedical proponents to engage with traditional medical systems in South Asia. For example, the Indian Medical Association (IMA) has strongly opposed allowing practitioners of Siddha, Ayurveda, and other alternative medical systems to practice modern medicine (Allopathy). In 2014, the Government of Maharashtra promulgated an ordinance permitting the AYUSH (Ayurveda, Yoga & Naturopathy, Unani, Siddha, Sowa Rigpa, and Homoeopathy) doctors to practice modern medicine (Allopathy). The Indian Medical Association strongly labelled it as "Government Sponsored Quackery." The statement of the IMA is of the following:

> Maharashtra Govt. has promulgated an Ordinance permitting AYUSH doctors to practice modern medicine. It is understood that the Governor has sent back the Ordinance without signing.
>
> When even a small shortcoming in treatment by qualified Doctor of Modern System of medicine is taken seriously with civil and criminal liabilities, what justification is there in this action of the Maharashtra Government.
>
> IMA should publicise this as a social evil, malpractice and should take it as a very serious issue. At the same time IMA, along with MCI, should give stringent directions to hospitals and doctors not to appoint AYUSH doctors as RMO / Assistants and strong action taken against those violating the directions.
>
> Indian Medical Association, 2014, December 27–28.

Indian Medical Association also defines quacks as follows:

(i) Quacks with no qualification whatsoever.
(ii) Practitioners of Indian Medicine (Ayurvedic, Siddha, Tibb, Unani), Homoeopathy, Naturopathy, commonly called AYUSH, who are not qualified to practice Modern Medicine (Allopathy) but are practicing Modern Medicine.
(iii) Practitioners of so-called integrated Medicine, Alternative System of Medicine, electro-Homoeopathy, Indo-allopathy, etc., terms which do not exist in any Act.

In 2015, the Indian Medical Association took a firm stance against AYUSH practitioners prescribing "modern medicine drugs" when the Union Government of India considered the possibility of permitting AYUSH practitioners by introducing a bridge course. Interestingly, many statements from the Indian Medical Association refer to "Allopathy" medicine exclusively as "modern medicine" and not other medical systems. Even the influential 167-page Indian Medical Council Act of 1956 (Government of India, 1956), which plays an essential role in regulating medical education and practice in India, mentions the term "modern" only twice. However, a single statement by the Indian Medical Association in 2015 titled "Ayush cannot prescribe modern medicine drugs" uses the word "modern" more than 20 times (IMA, 2015). This highlights the significant impact of the Bhore Committee Report of 1946 on the Medical Association of India and their understanding of what is considered scientific and what is not.

Not at the same level as the IMA, we have observed similar opposition to traditional medical systems in almost all the other South Asian countries. The medical doctors trained in biomedicine maintain similar views and attitudes to the Indian Medical Association in these countries.

3.5 Taking a Different Epistemology

Instead of promoting the traditional medical systems in South Asia, we attempt to bring a different epistemological understanding to health and wellbeing. In that, we are contrasting the single discipline analysis of the scientific methodology, which examines the human being as a separate entity from nature. Ancient medical systems such as Ayurveda, Siddha, and other traditional medical systems in South Asia are based on a shared yet unique set of principles. The key to understanding these principles is to realize that human beings are part of nature, and natural processes govern their constitution. These ancient traditions have a deep meaning in understanding the health and wellbeing of human beings. In that, the validation of knowledge processes, manifestation of diseases, the efficacy of treatment, and the development of new protocols are explained within different philosophical and classical texts (Lad, 2002; Manohar, 2012; Ministry of AYUSH, 2019; Murthy, 1991; Ram Manohar, 2006).

The epistemology and ontological vision of ancient traditional medical systems are based on a view that the universe is complex and based on philosophies (darshanas) of traditional systems of knowledge (Radhakrishnan, 1950, 1963). For example, Morandi (2021) explains that Ayurveda never has a beginning or end, and the only important aspect is for human beings to get to know and accept themselves and their position in nature.

The ancient methodological approaches that are embedded in South Asian traditional medical systems allow the practitioner's embodied experiences, which would enable a sensory negotiation between different epistemologies in the form of authoritative knowledge and technologies (Brooks, 2018). This is enacted as "epistemic virtues," which are internalized standards around effective means of knowledge and the forms of "disposition" that facilitate knowing (Daston & Galison, 2007). Brooks (2018) explains that, according to Ayurvedic practitioners, they use their bodies as instruments and tools, meaning they must live free from distractions. From a methodological perspective, this is commitment and compassion. Rather than understanding methodology as an external process, the methodology becomes a lifestyle.

3.5 Taking a Different Epistemology

Based on the South Asian traditional medical systems to facilitate health and wellbeing, we have identified the following dimensions as foundations within a different epistemology:

1. Spiritual.
2. Nature-centric.
3. Experiential.

Although these dimensions are presented here as three points, it is essential to understand that they are strongly interlinked. Spirituality can be understood as everything beyond the human physical limits. This idea is strongly connected to the point that all things on this planet, both living beings and non-living things, are interlinked. In return, there is a strong connection between individual physiology and nature. Humans are all connected with themselves, the people surrounding them, their immediate environment, and nature. This is what nature-centric means. Ancient South Asian philosophies claim that human beings are responsible for their choices and actions, which is experiential. In this understanding, there is no division between qualitative and quantitative, or induction or deduction. Ray (2010) argues that ancient science is subtler than modern science because modern science is often subject to statistical manipulation. While not arguing that the ancient approaches are better than modern scientific methods, we are proposing to establish equal collaborations for better learning for improved health and wellbeing within nature and natural processes. These possibilities and implications are further discussed in Chaps. 4 and 5.

Taking a different epistemological approach means identifying the complicated linkages of health and wellbeing within nature and sociocultural factors. In a modern sense, there is an increasing realization that nature and natural processes are the foundation of services that lead to health and wellbeing as they provide clean and nutritional resources, spiritual and recreational spaces, encouragement, and learning. This indicates the vitality of healthy ecosystems to ensure the health and wellbeing of individuals and communities. In contemporary perspectives, healthy ecosystems correlate to disease patterns, quality of life, and maintenance of an effective engagement of communities with their environments. The perspectives provided in ancient traditional medical systems in South Asia are not religious but practical for the survival of humans on this planet.

Given the increased natural hazards, diseases, and challenges due to the climate crisis, these ancient epistemological understandings are more than necessary in the contemporary world. In that, our proposal (see Chap. 6) is to overcome the divisions of knowledge through coloniality and capital marketplace and collaborate as equal partners for change.

References

Ahmad, K., Ahmad, M., Huber, F. K., & Weckerle, C. S. (2021). Traditional medicinal knowledge and practices among the tribal communities of Thakht-e-Sulaiman Hills, Pakistan. *BMC Complementary Medicine and Therapies, 21*, 1–21.

Arnold, D. (1993). *Colonizing the body: State medicine and epidemic disease in nineteenth-century India*. University of California Press.

Arnold, D. (2000). *Science, technology and medicine in colonial India* (Vol. 5). Cambridge University Press.

Barraclough, S. (2000). The politics of privatization in the Malaysian health care system. *Contemporary Southeast Asia, 22*, 340–359.

Borins, M. (1987). Traditional medicine in India. *Canadian Family Physician, 33*, 1061–1065.

Brooks, L. A. (2018). Epistemology and embodiment: Diagnosis and the senses in classical Ayurvedic medicine. *Asian Review of World Histories, 6*(1), 98–135.

Chari, P. S. (2003). Susruta and our heritage. *Indian J Plast Surg, 36*(4), 13.

Chattopadhyaya, D. (1978). *Science and society in ancient India* (Vol. 22). John Benjamins Publishing (Reprint of original 1977 edition).

Chokshi, M., Patil, B., Khanna, R., Neogi, S. B., Sharma, J., Paul, V. K., & Zodpey, S. (2016). Health systems in India. *Journal of Perinatology, 36*(3), S9–S12.

Chongsuvivatwong, V., Phua, K. H., Yap, M. T., Pocock, N. S., Hashim, J. H., Chhem, R., Wilopo, S. A., & Lopez, A. D. (2011). Health and health-care systems in Southeast Asia: Diversity and transitions. *The Lancet, 377*(9763), 429–437.

Crawford, S. C. (2001). Hindu bioethics for the twenty-first Century. *Journal of Hindu-Christian Studies, 14*(1), 9.

CRED. (2023). *2023 Disasters in numbers*. Centre for Research on the Epidemiology of Disasters (CRED).

Daston, L., & Galison, P. (2007). *Objectivity*. Zone Books.

Duggal, R. (1991). Bhore Committee (1946) and its relevance today. *The Indian Journal of Paediatrics, 58*, 395–406.

Gewali, M. B., & Awale, S. (2008). *Aspects of traditional medicine in Nepal*. Institute of Natural Medicine University of Toyama.

Government of India. (1956). The Indian medical council act, 1956. https://www.nmc.org.in/wp-content/uploads/2017/10/Complete-Act-1.pdf. Retrieved on December 05, 2023.

Guthrie, D. (1945). *A history of medicine*. T. Nelson and Sons.

Haque, M. I., Chowdhury, A. A., Shahjahan, M., & Harun, M. G. D. (2018). Traditional healing practices in rural Bangladesh: A qualitative investigation. *BMC Complementary and Alternative Medicine, 18*, 1–15.

Health Survey and Development Committee (Bhore Committee). (1946). *Report of the health survey and development committee, Vol II, recommendations*. Manager of Publications, Manager Government of India Press.

Hegde, B. M. (2015). Modern medicine: A trick or a trade? *Kuwait Medical Journal, 47*(3), 189–192.

Himanshu, Sharma, S., & Chugh, K. (2002). Sadvritta: Code of conduct in modern times. *World Journal of Pharmaceutical and Medical Research, 8*(10), 207–209.

Hussain, S., Malik, F., Khalid, N., Qayyum, M. A., & Riaz, H. (2012). Alternative and traditional medicines systems in Pakistan: History, regulation, trends, usefulness, challenges, prospects, and limitations. In A. Bhattacharya (Ed.), *A compendium of essays on alternative therapy*. InTech.

Indian Medical Association (IMA). (2014). Agenda Item No. A-2: Menace of Quackery. https://www.ima-india.org/ima/free-way-page.php?pid=199. Retrieved on December 05, 2023.

Indian Medical Association (IMA). (2015). Ayush cannot prescribe modern medicine drugs. https://ima-india.org/ima/archive-page-details.php?pid=245. Retrieved on May 27, 2024.

Jaiswal, Y. S., & Williams, L. L. (2017). A glimpse of Ayurveda-The forgotten history and principles of Indian traditional medicine. *Journal of Traditional and Complementary Medicine, 7*(1), 50–53.

References

Lad, V. (2002). *Textbook of Ayurveda: Fundamental principles of Ayurveda*. Ayurvedic Press.

Larson, G. J. (1987). Āyurveda and the Hindu philosophical systems. *Philosophy East and West, 37*(3), 245–259.

Loukas, M., Lanteri, A., Ferrauiola, J., Tubbs, R. S., Maharaja, G., Shoja, M. M., Yadav, A., & Rao, V. C. (2010). Anatomy in ancient India: A focus on the Susruta Samhita. *Journal of Anatomy, 217*(6), 646–650.

Macaulay, T. B. (1835). Minute by the Hon'ble T. B. Macaulay, dated the 2nd February 1835, Bureau of Education. In H. Sharp (Ed.), *Selections from educational records, Part I (1781–1839)*. Superintendent, Government Printing, 1920. Reprint. National Archives of India, 1965, 107–117.

Madhavan, V. R. (1984) *Siddha medical manuscripts in Tamil*. International Institute of Tamil Studies.

Manohar, P. R. (2012). Clinical evidence in the tradition of Ayurveda. In S. Rastogi, F. Chiappelli, M. H. Ramchandani, & R. H. Singh (Eds.), *Evidence-based practice in complementary and alternative medicine: Perspectives, protocols, problems and potential in Ayurveda*. Springer Science & Business Media.

McKay, A., & Wangchuk, D. (2005). Traditional medicine in Bhutan. *Asian Medicine, 1*(1), 204–218.

Mignolo, W. D. (2002). The geopolitics of knowledge and the colonial difference. *South Atlantic Quarterly, 101*(1), 57–96.

Mignolo, W. D. (2009). Epistemic disobedience, independent thought and decolonial freedom. *Theory, Culture & Society, 26*(7–8), 159–181.

Ministry of AYUSH. (2019). *Siddha system of medicine: The science of holistic health*. Government of India.

Morandi, A. (2021). Research methodology for Ayurveda and traditional systems of medicines: Practical difficulties and way ahead. *Journal of Ayurveda Case Reports, 4*(4), 128.

Mukherjee, P. K., Harwansh, R. K., Bahadur, S., Banerjee, S., Kar, A., Chanda, J., Biswas, S., Ahmmed, S. M., & Katiyar, C. K. (2017). Development of Ayurveda–tradition to trend. *Journal of Ethnopharmacology, 197*, 10–24.

Murthy, S. R. S. (1991). *Vagbhata. Ashtanga Hridaya*, English Translation. Chowkamba Press.

Narayanaswamy, V. (1981). Origin and development of Ayurveda: (a brief history). *Ancient Science of Life, 1*(1), 1.

Omran, A. R. (1998). The epidemiologic transition theory revisited thirty years later. *World Health Statistics Quarterly, 51*(2–4), 99–119.

Patwardhan, B., Deshpande, S., Tillu, G., & Mutalik, G. (2015). In search of roots: Tracing the history and philosophy of Indian medicine. *Indian Journal of History of Science, 50*(4), 629–641.

Phua, K. H. (1991). *Privatization & restructuring of health services in Singapore* (No. 5). Singapore: Institute of Policy Studies.

Pollock, S. (1989). Mīmāṃsā and the problem of history in traditional India. *Journal of the American Oriental Society, 109*(4), 603–610.

Radhakrishnan, S. (1950). *The Dhammapada: With introductory essays*, Pali Text, English Translation and Notes. Oxford University Press.

Radhakrishnan, S. (1963). *Bhagavad Gita*. George Allen and Unwin Ltd.

Rahman, H. M., & Hossen, A. M. (2017). Traditional medicinal practices in the context of Urban Bangladesh: Issues and challenges. *Society and Change, XI*(3), 21–36.

Rahmatullah, M., & Biswas, K. R. (2012). Traditional medicinal practices of a Sardar healer of the Sardar (Dhangor) community of Bangladesh. *The Journal of Alternative and Complementary Medicine, 18*(1), 10–19.

Ram Manohar, P. (2006). Evidence base for traditional medicine through practice-based research. In *International conclave on traditional medicine* (pp. 16–17).

Ravishankar, B., & Shukla, V. J. (2007). Indian systems of medicine: A brief profile. *African Journal of Traditional, Complementary, and Alternative Medicines: AJTCAM, 4*(3), 319–337.

Ray, A. (2010). *Yoga and Vipassana: An integrated lifestyle*. Inner Light Publishers.

Samhita, C. (1949). *Charaka Samhita. Vols I–VI.* Shree Gulab Kunverba Ayurvedic Society.
Sébastia, B. G. (2010). Treating diabetics with traditional medicine in Tamil Nadu: A study of two traditional siddha practitioners, article enseconde lecture dans le *Journal Anthropology and Medicine,* hal-00597057.
Shankar, D., Hafeel, A., Payyappapallimana, U., & Tagadur, S. (2003). Reviving local health traditions. In B. Haverkort, K. van't Hooft, & W. Hiemstra (Eds.), *Ancient roots, new shoots: Endogenous development in practice* (pp. 58–69). Zed Books.
Shaw, R., Luo, Y., Cheong, T. S., Abdul Halim, S., Chaturvedi, S., Hashizume, M., Insarov, G. E., Ishikawa, Y., Jafari, M., Kitoh, A., Pulhin, J., Singh, C., Vasant, K., & Zhang, Z. (2022). Asia. In H.-O. Pörtner, D.C. Roberts, M. Tignor, E.S. Poloczanska, K. Mintenbeck, A. Alegría, M. Craig, S. Langsdorf, S. Löschke, V. Möller, A. Okem, & B. Rama (Eds.), *Climate change 2022: Impacts, adaptation and vulnerability. Contribution of working group II to the sixth assessment report of the intergovernmental panel on climate change.* Cambridge University Press.
Sujatha, V. (2020). Globalisation of South Asian medicines: Knowledge, power, structure and sustainability. *Society and Culture in South Asia, 6*(1), 7–30.
Thirunarayanan, T. (1993). *An introduction to Siddha medicine.* Thirukumaran Publishers.
Tirtha, S. S. (2005). *The Āyurveda encyclopaedia: Natural secrets to healing, prevention & longevity.* Ayurveda Holistic Center Press.
Venkatraman, Dr. R. (1990). *A history of the Tamil Siddha cult.* Department of Art History, M.K. University Madurai.
Vicziany, M. (2021). The modernisation of South Asia's disease burden: 1950 to 2021. *South Asia: Journal of South Asian Studies, 44*(6), 1114–1130.
Weiss, R. S. (2009). *Recipes for immortality: Healing, religion, and community in South India.* Oxford University Press.
Weragoda, P. B. (1980). The traditional system on medicine in Sri Lanka. *Journal of Ethnopharmacology, 2*(1), 71–73.
White, D. G. (1997). *The alchemical body: Siddha traditions in medieval India.* University of Chicago Press.
World Bank. (2023). Population data: South Asia. https://data.worldbank.org/region/south-asia?view=chart. Retrieved on February 29, 2024.
World Health Organization. (2020). *Traditional medicine in the WHO South-East Asia region: Review of progress 2014–2019.* WHO.
Wujastyk, D. (2003). The science of medicine. In G. Flood (Ed.), *Wiley Blackwell companion to Hinduism,* pp. 399–413.
Wujastyk, D. (2008). The evolution of Indian government policy on ayurveda in the twentieth century. In D. Wujastyk, & F. M. Smith (Eds.), *Modern and global Ayurveda: Pluralism and paradigms.* State University of New York.
Zimmermann, M. (2001). *A short introduction: The Tamil siddhas and the siddha medicine of Tamil Nadu.* GRIN Verlag.

Chapter 4
Practical Implications and Possible Adaptations

4.1 Introduction

The mainstream scientific endeavour can be understood as an attempt to see an elephant through a keyhole. Scientists from various streams look through their keyholes—be it physics, biology, chemistry, or biomedicine. However, we argue that they fail to have a holistic view or understanding of being, nature, or the universe. Due to this, we find a deep problem in dissecting everything to pursue knowledge, which contradicts the holistic features of any beings and blurs our understanding. On the contrary, modern societies driven by Western biomedicine spend vast resources, time, and energy on science to understand the external world, particularly diseases. Despite this, the sufferings of human beings have not been controlled through these comforts and accessories.

In the contemporary period, modern societies invest ample time, resources, and vast amounts of energy in science and dissecting everything, aiming to understand the external world. How can we understand the beautiful smell of a flower by dissecting it? Or understand the life of a frog or bird by dissecting it? On the one hand, such "dissections" of the external world have generated more than enough comfort for the human populations in recent decades. However, as discussed in previous chapters, the sufferings of humans amidst these comforts and accessories have not been reduced—the risks that come from external factors such as environmental pollution, global warming, climate chaos, political instability, war, digital surveillance are on the rise, which resulted in rampant anxiety, depression, and many other mental sufferings among people both in the Global South and North. Also, infectious as well as non-communicable diseases are on the rise.

Improving individuals' health and wellbeing has become a source of suffering due to the dissection and externality. According to the great Indian saint Kabir Das, human happiness is found within and seeking it in the outside world is futile (Jhawar, 2004). Similarly, the Buddha explained that the individual is responsible for the harm and injury done to themselves, where these can only be undone by the individual; no one can do this for others (Dhammapada, Verse 165: Radhakrishnan, 1950, p. 114). The human organism (body and mind) is one of the most sophisticated organisms on this planet. We argue that human beings cannot experience living or existence without enhancing this organism. Understanding that our existence and living are within the planetary boundaries is essential. Humans must reconnect with nature, which governs this planet and its continuation.

4.2 Dying from Illness Versus Dying with Illness

Although not from South Asia, the following example from England shows the human ability to develop different understandings towards illnesses and dying. Janaka met Jennifer[1] in 2007 when she was a nurse at a General Practitioner (GP) practice, and immediately became family friends. She was kind and helpful to an immigrant family from Sri Lanka. Jennifer was accommodating when Janaka and his wife had their child, especially to understand the challenges in a different sociocultural context. This example is based on Janaka's conversations with Jennifer over the years:

> Jennifer was born into a poor mining family in North of England about 75-years ago. She worked hard to overcome poverty, so went to school and became a nurse. This was an achievement beyond her family's imagination. She is the first to go to university to get a degree. She was happy with her work and enjoyed meeting her patience and their families. After few years of her marriage, Jennifer started to experience violence and abuse from her husband. Through all the legal and social battles, Jennifer was left with her young daughter. However, she found her joy through her caring profession. "I am a nurse!" This was her identity as a human being. Her connection with other human beings were mostly praised by her colleagues, but there were times that some doctors did not like her caring, and compassionate nature. With all the life challenges, Jennifer managed to find her happiness through her work. Many years later, she met Paul, who is a kind-hearted man. They fall in love. Most importantly, Paul immediately became a father to Jennifer's daughter. They had a good life. Many years later, Jennifer made it – she got a comfortable house, and saved enough for her retirements. "I want to travel across England to see places", which was Jennifer's plan after retirement. On her 65th birthday Jennifer finally retired and was very excited to move on with her life. Now her daughter is grown-up and a professional with a young son. No worries! After about 5 years to her retirement, Jennifer started to have falls, which could not be explained. She broke her leg, arm, and after many tests, they diagnosed her with Parkinson. When she met the doctor, who she knew as a trainee many years ago said, "I am so sorry Jennifer, this is a life-long illness, and you will probably die from it." She thought for a moment, and replied to the doctor, "I will die with Parkinson, but I will not die from Parkinson."

In today's world, the burgeoning numbers of digital media and online medical platforms that are predominantly occupied by Western biomedicine experts provide a dual impact on people who are diagnosed with life-threatening illnesses. On the one hand, these platforms and experts disseminate knowledge on these diseases to the common public, including patients, and on the other hand, these platforms play potential roles in spreading fear and anxiety to them, which results in a good number of

---

[1] Name has been changed to protect the identity.

diagnosed patients die from fear or they succumb to the disease by losing their mental and physical strength over the period. Whereas Jennifer brought a very different perspective to her illness. Since she was diagnosed, Jennifer has been learning how to live with Parkinson's. She made life changes, which allowed her to live with it. As she realized that this is human nature, and it is inevitable to get illnesses. However, human nature is to learn how to live with these illnesses. By doing so, Jennifer found that she was not suffering from Parkinson's anymore.

Belle Monappa Hegde, often praised as the People's Doctor in South India, defines health as passion to work, and enthusiasm to be compassionate. In his small books (Hegde, 2019, 2021), he provides many cases of his own patients who were misguided by the health "scare" articles of the popular weeklies and even medical textbooks on diabetes titled such as "Genes play a vital role in diabetes and cancer and many of the modern-day killers" and "Doctors should be aware of the family history of a disease." Hegde is one of the famous allopathy doctors who voiced for decades that human genes only play a secondary role in transferring diseases from one generation to the next. According to him, the primary factors driving the illnesses are the environment and the lifestyle human's practice. He also puts a scathing critique against genetic scientists, saying that they exaggerate Darwinism and evolution theory. For that, they get grants and publish research papers in reputed scientific peer-reviewed journals. He is also one of the fervent advocates of Ayurveda and practising healing at home for many types of fevers (other than severe fevers such as Malaria) or coping with many diseases other than intense and terminal illnesses must ultimately be done by the body's immune system. In this context, it is also important to highlight that he had a mild stroke (the year is unknown), and then he was taken to the allopathy hospital, and he faced criticism because of his past censures to Western medicine. To respond to this, Hegde clarified that it is unwise to believe Ayurveda in times of emergency—for an emergency, Western biomedicine is the right option. His censures against Western biomedicine primarily focus on commercialization and less on preventing illnesses and environmental factors. We agree with him in this context that commercialization and compartmentalization of knowledge systems are some of the significant drawbacks of Western biomedicine. Throughout this book, we often use the term "Western Biomedicine." Beyond the technical definition provided by international institutions, we perceive this term highlights the establishment of institutional structures for the dominant medical profession within the Euro-North American context. In the contemporary world, Western biomedicine is grounded in Euro-North American epistemological and ontological foundations. This "grounded-ness" in the Euro-North American contexts distinguishes it from other forms of medicine and healing. Additionally, knowledge creators in biomedicine (researchers, academics, and textbook authors), along with advanced technology, have elevated the status of Western medical practice above other forms of medicine and healing. Consequently, Western biomedicine is understood as the "universal" theoretical framework for health science and health technology, developed in Euro-North American contexts and practised in healthcare settings and surrounding infrastructures.

As postulated by Ayurveda, Siddha, Deshiya Chikitsa, Unani, and many other South Asian traditions, the best healing motivation comes from the sick individual's mind. The ill individual can stimulate healing through personal belief, strength, or confidence in the treating doctor. Over the past few decades, Western biomedicine has taken the idea of health into the marketplace—the physician has become a salesperson for technology and pharmaceutical products, and the patient has become a consumer. This has transformed the honourable doctor–patient relationship, which complicates and sometimes, intensifies sufferings. In this context, it is equally important to highlight the fact that both Ayurveda and Siddha of South Asia have increasingly become commercialized in the recent decades, and both ancient medical systems are no more largely practiced in the way that it is used to be. Compared to Siddha, Ayurveda has largely commodified and commercialized in the past two decades (Singh & Gopal, 2016). Describing the industrial strategy of Ayurveda in Kerala, a state in India that predominantly still largely practises Ayurvedic medicines for various illnesses, Kudlu (2016) argues that the Ayurvedic industry in Kerala, primarily led and owned by traditional practitioners known as Vaidyans, evolved by supplying a range of medicines, constituting a pharmacopeia, to Ayurvedic doctors rather than engaging in competition. Thereby, it had successfully faced competition from Western biomedicine in the context of modernization and globalization. Also, it is vital to underline that the Ayurveda industry of Kerala projects Ayurvedic medicines as neither traditional nor modern—instead, it is being projected as powerful alternative, less-modern entities that can be embedded in both Ayurvedic traditional therapeutic frameworks and in the global marketplace.

Provided this, we invite the readers to examine health and wellbeing from a different angle critically. In general, we perceive that the Western biomedicine in the present form categorizes humans as a weak species as it gives less importance to humans' innate immunity systems and the surroundings that humans live in. In addition, nature has much to do with the evolution of this planet's living beings, which the Western biomedicine industry often fails to acknowledge. Along with this, on the other hand, several researchers of the Western world such as Bruce J. West have pointed out the limitations of "averages" of health indicators such as heart rate, body temperature, respiratory frequency, and highlight its fallacies in measuring health and wellbeing of the humans (For more: West, 2006, 2012). We believe it or not, several natural processes kept the human population surviving for so long without the assistance of medicine, science, and technology, which we can call as the innate intelligence of life.

As explained in Chap. 3, influential traditional medicinal systems such as Ayurveda and Siddha possess an understanding that an individual human being grounded in nature as a structural similarity between the human being and the cosmos as an integrated whole. In this, these health systems understood the importance of physical, mental, spiritual, and social wellbeing of humans, through balancing all the relationships an individual is placed into. Therefore, in several ways, unlike the contemporary Western biomedicine, ancient South Asian medical systems interventions are preventative and promotive, placing care of the sick individuals above cure. The reason for this is that the individual's actions determine the maintenance of a balanced relationship between health and illness, joy and suffering, and external and internal worlds. In these traditional approaches, there has always been

4.2 Dying from Illness Versus Dying with Illness

a strong emphasis on human responsibility—in these ways, health becomes more than medical interventions. Maintaining a total lifestyle would carry an individual from the cradle to the grave. Longevity is measured not by the number of years but by the quality of time. At the same time, the medical practitioner's effectiveness was understood within their capacity to prevent illnesses and diseases and not by their ability to cure. The following story that was told in different Asian countries explains this point:

> The king of the kingdom was ill from a disease that no one could cure. After many efforts, people found a doctor from a faraway village, and he was successful in his treatment. The king was so happy and wanted to honour the doctor with the title "the greatest doctor". However, the doctor refused to accept this honour. He said that I come from a family of doctors. My brother who is also a doctor can diagnose people at least 4-5 years before they become ill, and he treats them better. He is greater than me. But my sister, who is also a doctor, and when she sees an infant, she can tell how to prevent all the diseases they could get. She is the greatest doctor. The king was curious, and asked why don't we know about them? Because my brother and sister are so great that they prevent diseases. That is why you don't hear about them. I am a mediocre in my abilities, and I can only treat people when they fall ill. That is why people know about me, and not my siblings.

This shows the value of medical interventions from an ancient perspective, especially on promotive and preventative aspects. This also shows that health and wellbeing must not be placed within marketplace as a commodity. As we discuss further in this chapter, the mainstream health and wellbeing have become a commodity, which divides people between having access and not having access to healthcare. In this, the marketplace can only make money when people fall ill, and not by promoting healthy lifestyles or preventative approaches.

In the traditions of South Asian medical practices including Ayurveda and Siddha, life is understood to be the combination of human body, sensory organs, mind, and spirit. Both in Hindu and Buddhist perspectives, body is not simply a machine but the house for several components. For example, the body has the basic substances of earth, water, fire, air, and ether. The mind is localized in the body and produces consciousness. Ether is connected to *Poorna*—filled (in Hindu perspective) and *Shunya*—empty (in Buddhist perspective). Ether is what connect the human being to nature. In this, the human connection to the external world or surrounding happens through six sensory spheres opposed to the five sensory organs understood in biomedical sciences. They are:

1. Visibility through eyes.
2. Sound through ear.
3. Odour through nose.
4. Taste through tongue.
5. Touch through skin (or body).
6. Mental objects through mind.

Mind is treated as a sensory organ as it interacts with sense objects that includes impressions, feelings, perceptions, and decision-making.

These forms the human being that represents three expressions of life. The body or material forces are involved in the maintenance of a state of physical health of balance of all expressions of human organisms, and their restoration when unstable. The mind cultivates an approach to life. When ignorance in the mind is removed, one can achieve wellbeing. Various South Asian approaches such as Ayurveda and Siddha, to health and wellbeing facilitate the body and mind to maintain a balanced state. This process is conducted by coordinating and harmonizing the human being for a joyful material existence, proper earthly conduct, and motivation for understanding of the true relationship between human, their world, and the ultimate source of their consciousness and existence. These perspectives cannot be ignored as "unscientific" or romantic ideas anymore. Over the past 100 years or so, we have seen that the capital marketplace has produced a blend of more success in physical health but more failures in ensuring wellbeing of humans. For example, the invention of vaccines have prevented threatening diseases such as polio and smallpox in almost all regions of the world. While this is a resounding success in reducing mortality rates and physical health and wellbeing worldwide, we have also recently seen how the wealthy countries stocked vaccines without sharing with poor nations across the world during the COVID-19 pandemic.

4.3 Ancient Understanding(s) and Modern Tensions

Ancient medicinal systems such as Ayurveda and Siddha traditionally possess an understanding health is not absolute, and every science has its limitations. Both medicinal systems do not promise for permanently and absolutely free from diseases and sufferings. In that, medicine and herbs depend on seasons, timing, and so many other factors. Health is all about involvement within the human body, as well as their surroundings. If there is no involvement, the subtle aspects of life will disappear. Involvement is not domination, but collaboration with compassion, humility, and care. This means that living is paying attention to everything and be attentive. Ayurveda, Siddha, and Deshiya Chikitsa historically possess strong understanding that health as a matter of continual fine-tuning to maintain health and wellbeing. The reason for this understanding is that human beings are always sick because life itself is impermanent and going through transition. An infant becomes a child, and then move into teenage years. The young then grow old. These are unavoidable transitions in life, which make life unstable. There is always some disease attracting the human being, particularly in changes of life circumstances or external changes of seasons. The South Asian philosophies always understand that each living being that is born must eventually die. This is the natural process that ancient wisdoms understand.

The organ-based treatments or quick-fix in biomedicine alone cannot bring health, healing, and wellbeing. Health is a holistic process where the "healthy turmoil" must be restored to attract human beings into the "vibrant health attractor" and prevent them from getting attracted by the "stagnant death attractor" (Firth, 1991). Even in medical research, it has been explained that very strict control of blood sugar may increase the possibilities of death among critically ill patients (Watkinson et al., 2006). The ancient wisdoms from South Asia understood that human body is a complex living

4.3 Ancient Understanding(s) and Modern Tensions

being. Every cell and organ in the body has a job to do—to keep the body alive. That happen when each and every cell in the body is functioning well. The linear thinking of biomedical approaches only focuses on one organ. The heart specialist, lung specialist, brain specialist, and many other specialists that are concentrating on one organ are highly incapable of healing or facilitating health and wellbeing of human beings. This is like patching a torn piece of cloth with strong thread. It is torn piece of cloth anyway, even after patching. This applies to human health and life as well. The following anecdote explains, Janaka's personal experience of the application of healing by a traditional medical practitioner in Sri Lanka:

> During 1981, we were living in Colombo district, and this was a period that I have seen my mother falling ill. First it all started as allergic reactions to various food. At the end she could only eat rice and coconut milk curry. Then to make things worse, my mother started to develop a terrible knee pain where she could not walk, stand, or sleep. So, we kept going to many different medical practitioners – from western medical doctors to traditional medical practitioners. This went on for many months without a solution. In one instance, we went to a Buddhist Monk who was a traditional Sri Lankan medical practitioner (Deshiya Chikitsa).[2] The Buddhist Monk's medical centre was a fascinating place for me. Mainly because of various herbs around and they were making various chemical drinks, powders, and ointments. The person who was in charge was mixing all these different herbs according to the instructions of the Monk and giving them to patients in bottles and packets. Then I was fascinated by the long discussion the Monk had with us. He was taking notes of our family structure, problems we were facing, and specific issues my mother had within the family. Then he told something that I only understood later in my life. He said, *"there are various memories in our bodies. Brain related memory is what everyone knows. But there is memory in our five senses separately, as well as there is Karmic memory, and they can create these allergies."* As I understood, the Monk diagnosed my mother's condition as something to do with her memory, which had nothing to do with her brain. She started to get better slowly.

The other essential aspect for health and wellbeing is prevention. Mainstream Western biomedical approaches to health pays very little attention to maintenance and promotion of health. Although, the World Health Organization (WHO) and many national health services discuss about healthy populations, there is very little or very minimal resources allotted by the rich countries to promote health. To keep a society tranquil and promoting its health could only be achieved through proper education of the future generation. However, what we see in many developed and developing societies are the children who are suffering from many physical and mental ailments. Healthy eating, well-adjusted physicality, disease-resisting immune system, balanced lifestyle, and ability to effectively deal with external challenges must be taught from the childhood. The core of Ayurveda says:

Swasthasya Swasthya rakshanam

(Try to preserve the health of the healthy)

(Godbole et al., 2016, p. 415)

One could argue that screening populations routinely for illnesses and diseases has been done as a preventative method and therefore promoting health. However,

---

[2] https://ayudeptncp.lk/en/featured/deshiyachikithsa/.

linear model for deterministic predictability has a major problem. As argued by Prasad et al. (2016), this has resulted in most, if not all, medical data, being questionable. Biomedical approaches have been predicting the unpredictable future of human beings by screening the apparently healthy individuals and declaring them to be unhealthy while ignoring the fact that living organisms are nonlinear and any dynamic system will have unpredictable behaviour based on the history and environment (Firth, 1991). In the case of human beings, this is based on their genes, mind, and body. Routine screening could only measure a few factors of the human body. Stewart-Brown and Farmer (1997) argued that screening could seriously damage one's health, however, help the medical and pharmaceutical industry to make profits.

Human beings are different from all other animals on this planet, because their mind can influence their brains and all other organisms. The Bhagavad Gita (Radhakrishnan, 1963) explains that human beings are unique from the rest of the animal kingdom that they can make decisions on what is right and wrong (intellect). The new scientific inventions have been possible because of their capacity to think. At the same time, human beings are frustrated with the attractions to this world while getting attached to them. They are distressed by the contradictory dynamics of this world yet devoting themselves to their own personalities. There are many studies that explain the significant role of the mind in relation to many physical illnesses such as cancer, and heart attacks (Balon, 2006; Gidron & Ronson, 2008; Krantz et al., 2000; Ray, 2004). Similarly, scientific studies have also shown that patients with heart disease have shown poor outcomes in negative emotional states. Positive psychology states such as optimism, happiness, and altruism provide positive responses and interventions to the patients with heart diseases (Gidron & Ronson, 2008).

In recent years, though research by premier Western institutes has provided emphasis on positive psychology states and their influence on health and well-being, we should also note that its importance has not been widely disseminated. Even today, mainstream allopathy medical fields give more importance to research related to cures, not prevention, and improving the quality of the sound environment. Unfortunately, over the past few decades, the mainstream education systems in most developing nations such as in South Asia do not include any facilitation of learning among students of the art of living or their ability to deal with external challenges. The basis of most distress arises from frustration in life. This is mainly because human beings expect more than they need. They want more and more from life beyond their capacities. Institutionalized education needs to teach students to be satisfied with what we have or are. When humans expect to achieve something beyond their abilities and fail to achieve what they want, they get distressed. The Buddhist perspective of competition explains how people become distressed:

Jayam veram pasavati dukkhani set parajito

Upasanto sukham seti hitva jayaparajam

Victory breeds hatred; the conquered dwells in sorrow. They who have given up thoughts of both victory and defeat, calm and lives happily.

Dhammapada, Verse 201

Radhakrishnan (1950, p. 126)

4.3 Ancient Understanding(s) and Modern Tensions

Since our mainstream education is increasingly becoming competitive and it aims to make students to score more marks in exams, in general, it does not make any effort to facilitation of collaboration, compassion, and care for each other. From the beginning to the graduation from universities, students are being taught to compete with each other. Then, when these individuals come into the wider society, their default position is to compete and expect high achievements. This is one reason for jealousy and hatred when one sees their colleagues are doing better than themselves. In the capital marketplace, lives are busy and need to work hard to climb the professional ladder. There is hardly any time for near and dear ones. No one rarely has time for themselves or others.

Quick-fixed medical interventions through Western biomedical approaches such as medicine, psychotherapy, and counselling may give short-term solutions at the individual levels. However, to find lasting solutions for the society at large comes within the humans collectively and radical changes have to happen in our current environments. Human beings must think for themselves and work on themselves. Considering that the human being is the manager of their own body, both physical, mental, and spiritual, they need to think and act as a manager who wants to be joyful. What we have been learning is to manage ourselves so badly where we become distress and in the long run to become unhealthy. In return, the Ayurvedic tradition had the wisdom that the mind can influence all diseases. According to Charak Samhita, a leading Ayurvedic text, anger, greed, fear, jealousy, grief, extreme exhaustion, sedentary lifestyle, and many other things disturb the equilibrium of body and mind (Kumar et al., 2020). There is also the remedy to bring balance to the body and mind. Moderation food intake, work hard, avoid hatred, lies, and backstabbing, be courageous to even forgive the enemy, always judge any issue afterwards, and most importantly, love all beings in this world as your own (Kutumbiah, 1962). Similarly, in Buddhist philosophy, which Deshiya Chikitsa in Sri Lanka is based on, the Dhammapada clarifies that greed and self-indulgence are the worst among all illnesses, and attachment creates the utmost sorrow (Radhakrishnan, 1950, Verse 203, p. 126). The Bhagavad Gita points out that the passage to liberation is not for the human that is indulging in too much food or eating too little, oversleeping, or sleeping less (Radhakrishnan, 1963). To overcome all sorrows, one must practice moderation in food, and recreation, regulated sleep and waking, and control in own action, which establishes self-discipline. To be satisfied or fulfilled with what you gain is very important for a healthy lifestyle.

Not only in South Asia, but native people in North America also knew about the importance of the balance between body and mind. On the other hand, it is also equally noteworthy that current mental health and therapeutic practices do not work well with native Americans (Graham & Thomas 2002; Weaver, 2004). Anishinaabeg people occupy the territories in the Southeast of Canada and Northeast of the United States of America (Hele, 2020). Their philosophical thought point towards a path towards mino-bimaadiziwin. Although, many translations refer to this word as "good life", according to Sinclair (2013), this is somewhat deceptive as the word has many more meanings. Mino-bimaadiziwin is the foundational principle in which laws like the Seven Sacred Teachings (often called the Seven Grandfather's Teachings) were formed. These teachings are: Nibwaakaawin (Wisdom), Zaagi'idiwin (Love), Minaadendamowin (Respect), Aakode'ewin (Bravery), Gwayakwaadiziwin (Honesty), Dabaadendiziwin (Humility), Debwewin (Truth), (Sinclair, 2013, p. 61). Before the arrival of European colonizers, Anishinaabeg people did not suffer from major illnesses and lived far beyond one hundred years (Garro, 1990). However, Anishinaabeg people are suffering from all the major illnesses and diseases that any other European Canadian or European American gets. For native Americans, spirituality is centre to wellness (Gilgun, 2002; Lowery, 1998). Whereas the mainstream Western mental health and therapeutic practices largely overlooks the spiritualistic elements of native Americans to their wellbeing as they are often in the garb of secular outlook. Recognizing the ineffectiveness of the mainstream approaches and its implicit colonial nature, Hodge et al. (2009), recommends for the therapeutic and mental health practices that are constructed in the Native practice modalities from the ground up. They argue for the native presuppositional foundations rather than Enlightenment presuppositional foundation. Hence, our argument on emphasizing.

All South Asian traditional medical systems point towards the importance of eating natural and seasonal food, getting up early and going to bed early, hard physical activities, and closely observing the natural processes, especially based on the sun and moon cycles. There are many research reports, articles, and books written about the Circadian rhythm, which is key to living healthy and maintaining wellbeing. Of course, this does not mean that everything and everyone was enjoying the highest level of health and wellbeing in ancient South Asia; however, there was a better understanding of nature and natural processes.

In terms of the bigger picture of health, it has a lot to do with the current capital marketplace. The gap between the rich and poor are widening at an alarming rate. According to the World Health Organization (WHO, 2023), there are 1.9 billion adults that are overweight or obese, while 462 million adults are underweight. Similarly, the World Health Statistics Report (WHO, 2022) provides a disturbing picture of global health. Deaths from non-communicable diseases (NCDs) increased from 61% in the year 2000 to almost 74% in 2019. Communicable diseases such as TB, HIV, malaria, hepatitis B, and various overlooked tropical diseases are continued to give huge burden to low- and middle-income countries. Nearly half of all deaths are caused by these preventable or manageable diseases. This huge mortality rates could easily be reduced by addressing the developmental disparities of these nations. We could bring down two billion infections, twenty-five million incapacitation, five million visual impairments, and many other health issues in low and middle-income nations if those people have adequate access to clean drinking water, sanitation, and hygiene (Prüss-Üstün et al., 2008). The poor pay for their poverty with their lives. Poverty can also be understood as the mother of all human illnesses. Along with this, global warming and temperature rise threaten the very existence of humans and non-humans' survival and collapse the overall balance of this earth. In all probability, climate change is already a threat. In the future, the effects of climate change will be unprecedented—importantly, a large portion of poor and marginalized sections of South Asians will have to bear the adverse effects of climate change.

4.3 Ancient Understanding(s) and Modern Tensions

What is clear from the data is that most health challenges can be overcome by improving the living standards of the poor. However, it has become clear over the past 100-years that the linear analysis of poverty and implementing neoliberal policies in the capital marketplace will not largely improve the living conditions of the poor. Several scholars over the past few decades have already critiqued the inadequacy of the mainstream development paradigm which is based on linear and narrow economics and technocratic approaches (Friedman, 2003; Prashad, 2014; Wignaraja, 1991). However, most critiques are still at the margins of the discourse. In addition, these critiques are fragmented, and they focus on only specific aspects of the challenges. The early integration of "social" to "economic" development by neoliberal reformists, and the replacement of "human" development, do not effectively integrate planetary systems—most importantly, it fails to integrate natural processes into the discourse. Mainstream development policies driven by a capitalistic approach failed to address the emerging fundamental contradictions that are continuing to deepen in global realities (Sianipar, 2008; Sullivan & Hickel, 2023). Despite the decolonization achieved by colonial nations politically, widespread negligence prevails amongst the low- and middle-income nations in addressing the Sustainable Development Goals (SDGs) agenda. The decision-making process in the governance systems of these nations would require much clarity. Despite political decolonization, several low- and middle-income countries' mainstream development models have been mainly shaped by Western (or external) intellectual forces rooted in Euro-North American ideologies and a global imperialistic agenda. The poor and marginalized of these countries have little or no control over these policies and development models. Hence, continuity and imitation of these external models continue to dominate both the development discourse and political decision-making processes of these countries rather than meaningfully engaging the local communities in development agenda and to addressing the social, economic, and environmental challenges of these marginalized populations. Friedman (2003) explains that the capital marketplace has motivated people to compete with each other at every level, which has devastating impacts on everything from health to education to moral standards. In this process, humans have invented new approaches, theories, and frameworks of anger, hatred, and discrimination towards each other in the name of nationality, religion, security, cast, class, colour, and many other domains. This means that humans are at crossroad to move into nonlinear development agenda for improving living standards of everyone and create the space for humanity as the foundation of our societies. In short, we humans have failed to learn less from the inadequacies of the past. We need to make a transformative shift from our current thinking to address these issues—merely reassessing the challenges of poverty and reviewing our past actions are not enough to address them. Moreover, this transformative shift in thinking should keep nature, health, and wellbeing at the core. We need to acknowledge the limitations of our planetary boundaries and consider the objective forces of history that made us stay in this position. At the heart of it, as we said already, this transformation requires collective consciousness, where people recognize their inherent creativity and the need to create wealth and prosperity while engaging with nature in a balanced way. For this, we need to look at our ancient philosophical traditions, including Hindu, Buddhist,

Mayan, Ubuntu, and Pagan traditions—they offer valuable insights into how humans can harmonize their physical, mental, and spiritual processes with the natural world. These traditions emphasize a holistic approach to life, fostering wellbeing and a sustainable relationship with nature and the environment.

We argue that establishing a collaboration between Euro-North American philosophies and Ancient South Asian philosophies to reintroduce nature into health and wellbeing requires a major transformation in thinking. When two knowledge systems or epistemologies have different powers or dominating capacities, there is no space for collaboration as equal partners. In the discourse of health and wellbeing, the dominance of Western biomedicine is visibly apparent, and it is too difficult to learn from ancient philosophical understandings of health and wellbeing in this imbalanced power, which is why we argue for transformation.

4.4 Transformation—A Possibility?

The word "transformation" has often been used in many global discourses—in several subjects. What we witness in the recent decades is that there is a massive push for transformation in health, climate change, education, and many other areas tailoring to the rapid changes that are occurring in the contemporary world. What, then, is transformation? There is no consensus amongst scholars and policymakers to define the term "transformation." Most acknowledge that transformation implies a more fundamental change than the "old system." Nevertheless, we argue that this simplified understanding of "transformation" is inadequate and does not provide meaningful understanding. We argue that transformation negates the previous state completely and emerges into a new change—in which it does not contain any remainder of the previous state (Pillay, 2019). Butzer (2012) argues that it is a consequence of the collapse of a system and, therefore, negative. Folke et al. (2010) argue that transformation is the ability to change an essential element of a functioning system. Feola (2015) finds that the term "transformation" is frequently used merely as a metaphor. The lack of consensus about what transformation is and what it should be is the topic of research and debate. When do we call change transformational? We need to answer the important questions about what transformational processes entail (Jayawickrama, 2010; Pillay, 2019).

Instead of the transformation of the mainstream healthcare system, which is based on biomedical sciences, we argue that the change should begin at the individual level. Hence, we argue for the need for individual transformation. For example, let us take a medical doctor trained in India, Sri Lanka, Nepal, Bangladesh, or Pakistan. The curriculum that the medical students follow is essentially based on biomedical sciences, and hence, we cannot find radical difference in both academics and practice settings. Initially, they learn internal medicine (including cardiology, dermatology, neurology, venereology, and sexually transmitted infections), surgery and related subspecialties (including anaesthesiology, ophthalmology, orthopaedic surgery, and

4.4 Transformation—A Possibility?

otorhinolaryngology), obstetrics and gynaecology, psychiatry, paediatrics, community medicine, and family medicine. Given the study period, study load, and study pressure, medical students do not have time or space, or, most importantly, the expertise of their teachers, to learn traditional medical approaches in their own countries. As we know well, most medical curriculums in all these countries do not include modules that facilitate compassion, care, listening, or humility.

As we argue, mainstream education does not facilitate students to develop their abilities to deal with external challenges. The qualification-based education focuses on compartmentalized learning and not a holistic understanding of life. Whether the student becomes a scientist, artist, or some other professional, they do not have an understanding of their connection to nature or natural processes. In this, we argue that a total transformation of individuals and their learning is needed to reintroduce nature into health and wellbeing. Here is the challenge. Suppose the individual must transform for the system to transform. In that case, there should be some acknowledgment and awareness that this process is essential to understanding health and wellbeing transformation. For this, we propose the importance of introducing at least one or two compulsory courses that discuss these topics rooted in traditional medical systems of their own countries/regions.

Max-Neef (1991) explain the inability of political thoughts and development styles to connect with personal transformation. Humans have reduced themselves to consumers, clients, professionals, or beneficiaries, which does not facilitate any space for personal growth or transformation. However, Max-Neef argued that wider transformation is interconnected to personal transformation. He explains that a "healthy society should advocate above all the development of every person and of the whole person" (1991, p. 59).

Our mainstream education that is being taught in school and universities are actually grounded in Euro-North American philosophical systems. It teaches us that the physical world operates according to observable, measurable, objective, and universal principles. We, humans, who get education from this system, in turn, seek mastery over these principles to exert greater control over the world for our benefit (Jayawickrama, 2010; Pillay, 2019). Markley and Harman (1982) present that different knowledge systems provide different standards of understandings, and it is therefore not possible to prove that one is better than the other. Against, what has been promoted as universal scientific knowledge, biomedical sciences are not different to Ayurveda, Deshiya Chikitsa, Siddha, and many other medical systems in South Asia. Thomas Kuhn, one of the prominent American philosophers argued that the Euro-North American paradigm of reality can no longer include the limits of human knowledge, and he argued for the need for transformation in health and wellbeing (Kuhn, 1962).

Perspectives of transformation can be understood within the theory of health as expanding consciousness (Newman, 2000). What is important to note here that this theory originates not from medical sciences, but from a unitary and transformative perceptions of nursing. What Newman (2007) observed is that, as medical technology advances, there is a great need of a caring connection between nurses and patients. However, due to treatment-focused interventions from a biomedical perspective, nurses cannot establish those connections. The foundation of Newman's (2007) idea can be summarized as follows:

1. Health can be understood as an evolving singular pattern of the whole, including patterns of diseases.
2. Consciousness can be understood within the evolving pattern, which is the informational capacity of the whole.
3. Pattern can be understood by meaning and identified the human-environment process.

Pattern or design plays an important part in Newman's theory. Pattern represents the information that portrays the whole or entirety. The transformation of pattern happens within the patient-environment interaction, or the way which the patient connects with nature.

As derived from nursing, Newman's theory of health as expanding consciousness is an important example, how health and wellbeing can be understood differently from biomedical scientific understanding through linear analysis. Nurses are primarily focusing on care of people when they are experiencing chaos in their lives due to diseases or illnesses. Caring as a concept can be operationalised through compassion, humility, and collaboration. This is different to what medical doctors deliver through treatment-focused health interventions. In their engagement with a patient, nurses get to see the individual as a whole and meaning of healing in the experience. While most traditions of healing in South Asia does not divide between the doctoring and nursing, many practitioners of Ayurveda, Deshiya Chikitsa, and Siddha consider their patients as a whole within their environment and manage to facilitate a healing experience. For example, Wolf and Abell (2003, pp. 9–10), who is one of the transformative coachers who has experience in Vedic philosophy explains on the approach of a Vedic social worker towards the needy clients:

> More precisely, a Vedic social worker seeks to help clients uncover knowledge that is within. This conception of a priori knowledge contrasts the interpretivist paradigm. A Vedic therapist considers understanding the feelings and perceptions of the client as being very important, but more for the purposes of gaining trust and demonstrating caring, than from the ontological framework that client subjectivity represents truth.

Although, there are many similar perspectives that have emerged, and emerging in the health and wellbeing discourse, there remains the unavoidable challenge. That is that health and wellbeing remain in the marketplace and driven by profits rather than promoting health and preventing diseases. From our point of view, this remains one of the biggest, if not the main barrier for transformation of health and wellbeing within nature.

4.5 Implications for Transformation

Ancient philosophies from South Asia – Hindu, Buddhist, Jain, and other philosophies can be understood as a flowing like strands of braided hair, collecting from a single consciousness of generations. According to Ryser (1997), the apparent division between personal and collective identity is merely an illusion resulting from physical separation. He argues that; *"the personal self is to the collective self as the upstream waters are to the full rivers below* (p. 1)." Similarly, the following story explains that there is a tension between the modern scientific understanding of life, and ancient understandings of life and living. The following story shows the tension between tradition and modernity but also the tension between the differences in epistemologies:

> In the Amazon rain forest, a Cofan Indian elder conversed with a "gringo" from the "world beyond the forest." The elder's knowledge of the rain forest surpassed that of biologists holding PhDs, who came to study there. His was a practical knowledge. He is able to find and identify more than 140 plants his people used for medicinal purposes. He knows where the peach tree grows and when its fruit attracts the brilliant blue gold macaw. In addition to his knowledge, the elder has access to a great research library. Each volume is a friend. That woman over there, she knows all there is to know about marital discord and how to ensure a household's harmony. That old man walking beneath the trees, he talks to the God of Creation. The brothers fishing along the strand, they are the heads of a family that has built the best boats on the river for many generations. The elder's material possessions are scant and include a machete from upriver and two cloaks from the city. His wife owns several spoons and a metal pot. Aware of the village school, run by a Jesuit priest, the visitor asks, *"Do any of your children go on to high school in the city? Do any seek a university education?"*
>
> The old man shakes his head. There is too much to be learned at home. *"It takes many years to learn to be a Cofan,"* he says. His gaze drifts across the river, then returns to the gringo. *"My heart aches for you,"* he says. *"For me?"* replies the gringo. *"Why?" "Because you are so poor. We in the forest have all we want. You gringos want for so much you do not have."*
>
> Henning, (2002, p. 170)

This tension between the Euro-North American epistemologies and ancient wisdoms are not just anecdotal. Different epistemologies have been practiced in different parts of the world. This means that there are different understandings of the world beyond Euro-North American understandings. The mainstream epistemology derive from Euro-North American context have excluded and discriminated many societies everywhere must be understood against the historical record of colonialism, global capital marketplace, and institutions. The mainstream development discourse is and has been based on this Euro-North American epistemology, which is about happy with money. As discussed by Miñarro et al. (2021), who analyzed subjective wellbeing in low-income nations with different monetization levels, wellbeing is not necessarily linked with economic development. They revealed that indigenous communities with no sophisticated material and technological prosperity but are highly connected with nature scored a happiness score of over 8 points, surpassing Finland at 7.9 average—the highest among OECD countries. These findings, which essentially point towards the provision of basic needs, access to healthy natural surroundings, and social cohesion as drivers of wellbeing, are missing in the mainstream discourse of health and wellbeing.

The wisdoms of people of the rest of the world before Euro-North American hegemony towards nature were different and looking back into history, we can speculate that in general, they emphasized for harmonious relationship with nature but not to conquer nature. For example, The Bhagavad Gita, Chap. 3, verse 27, observes that the grace of nature governs every human activity, and only arrogant people deny that (Radhakrishnan, 1963, p. 143). The understanding is that nature is the main ruler of every human activity. This means that destroying nature will affect its regular processes and activities, which in return will affect the human beings living. There is a warning to arrogant people who do not realize the power of nature. In Chap. 7, verses 4–6, the Bhagavad Gita focuses on the relationship between humans and the environment (Radhakrishnan, 1963, pp. 2013–215) whereby the responsibility of the human, with mind, intelligence, and senses, is to maintain a position of balance and health with the other elements of nature such as land, water, air, and space. In the end, the harmonious relationship between humans and nature helps all of the world to flourish.

The ancient Chinese philosophy, Taoism shares the same viewpoint of inclusivity, or non-dualism. In Chap. 42, the Tao Te Ching claims, "the Tao gives birth to One. One gives birth to Two. Two gives birth to Three. Three gives birth to everything." (Zhihua, 2012, p. 279). This means humans have the same origins as everything. Zhihua (2012) claims that according to Taoism, the planet and human beings not only have the same origin and nature but also share the same structure and law. Based on this perspective, Taoist philosophy has a deeper understanding of the human's close dependence on the environment. Maintaining a harmonious relationship between humans and nature is a requirement for human life on this planet. From a more practical perspective, Mencius, a Chinese Confucian philosopher (372–289 BCE) called for environmental consciousness, the conservation of forests and waters, and for diversified livelihoods as ways to enhance the quality of life as well as maintaining a harmonious relationship with the environment (Rainey, 2010). The Southern African philosophy of Ubuntu brings similar values. According to Tutu (2004), the personhood is constructed in Ubuntu philosophy based on their relationships to others, to community, structures, and learning. The conclusion is that humans need each other to be fully human and must live in harmony with nature (Wright & Jayawickrama, 2021). Within this Ubuntu philosophy, one of the most important aspects is interaction with nature (Mbiti, 1991). A nourishing environment provides human beings with resources. Living in harmony with nature is inevitable because human beings are totally dependent on natural processes such as sun, rain, and winds (Mbiti, 1991). The Karaniya Metta Sutta—Buddhist Hymn of Universal Love (Buddharakkhita, 1989) aspires towards all beings living as joyful and secure, happy within themselves, without any exception, movable or immovable, long, or huge, medium, or small, subtle, or gross, visible, or invisible, residing far or near, born, or coming to birth. This aspiration or the wish comes from a realization that the individual human being is connected to all beings, including trees and plants on

4.5 Implications for Transformation

this planet. Any harm to them will affect the individual, so they not only aspire but work toward the protection of all living beings.

The major implication for reintroducing nature into health and wellbeing is that humans have established a conflict with nature (Smith & O'Keefe, 1980), whereby we intend to dominate it in pursuit of our capitalistic goals. This Euro-North American, dualistic separation, O'Keefe (2020) points towards that results in no life at all as we accept that all of life is not within one-self and, therefore, rational pursuits are namely to purchase commodities from the capital marketplace. This line of thinking, which flows from the Ancient Greeks to Rene Descartes to Adam Smith, and ultimately to linear scientific analysis and concepts of logical positivism, in other words from Euro-North American knowledge systems, creates the contemporary worldview (Jayawickrama, 2023; Zelinsky, 1975). Smith and O'Keefe (1980) point out that positivist tradition dominates mainstream science including the discourse of health and wellbeing, and this tradition inherently assumes that nature exists in and for itself, external to us and our activities. Stated succinctly, the result is a worldview in which the human population exists separate and outside of nature. As discussed by Smith and O'Keefe (1980), the production of nature in the capital marketplace was developed internationally, through political and military means. In the capital marketplace, nature is to be dominated. It is to be controlled, manipulated, and produced for its economic value rather than its intrinsic worth. They further explained that science has already become a commodity and comes with a price. Smith and O'Keefe (1980) argued that behind the domination of nature is the production of nature as sole reality. In this the sacredness of nature, as ancient civilisations beyond Europe understood it, is of no economic value and therefore abandoned as a rational pursuit. The scientific worldview and knowledge system we know today evolved in result or as a result of this process (O'Keefe, 2020; Smith & O'Keefe, 1980).

Within the current marketplace, humans are producing nature through urbanization, rapid infrastructure development, monoculture systems of agribusiness, and by replacing animal habitats with human settlements (Smith & O'Keefe, 1980). In this process of production of nature, people have changed their relationship to nature from an organic and harmonious one to a controlling one, which is never fully achieved because nature remains far above human capabilities (Jayawickrama, 2023). People also changed their relationships with themselves and each other as individuals through the creation of divisions and controlling measures. Science and technology of our period are expected to address global challenges like climate change. Whereas in reality, it further intensifies our risks and vulnerabilities at multiple fronts.

This means that the overall linear scientific analysis, which flows from Euro-North American knowledge, is an insufficient methodology for addressing contemporary risks and challenges (O'Keefe, 2020; Smith & O'Keefe, 1980; Zelinsky, 1975). This analysis shows that isolating a few factors from complex social realities makes them abstract, and social aspects are secondary to science. Separation of the researcher from the subject—emphasizing independence, impartiality, and neutrality—cannot produce meaningful understanding and experiences of the subject under study. In reality, strict objectivity is difficult to justify, mainly when the aim is to bring a 'change' to the context.

4.6 Disobeying Euro-North American Epistemology

When Janaka started his work as a humanitarian worker in 1990s, he was always asked to talk about his experiences from Sri Lanka in international, workshops and seminars. Although he has worked in India, Nepal, and Bangladesh at that time, it was pointed that as a Sri Lankan, he should talk about his own country, and not South Asia. During the hype of decolonisation debates in the UK, Janaka was asked many times to refrain from talking about racism in contexts other than Sri Lanka. By this time, Janaka has been collaborating and working in countries from Asia, Africa, Europe, and West Asia. It was told many times, that he can only represent his own Sri Lankan culture—he is a token of his culture! As the experience go with both Janaka and Devendraraj in different international platforms, such expectations will not appear if the scholar comes from Europe or North America. As Mignolo (2009) observes, in many cases, it is not assumed that one must be talking about their own culture but can function as a theoretically minded person. The European and North American societies have science and knowledge. The rest of the world has culture and wisdom. Like Mignolo (2009), we have wondered why the Euro-North American ways of knowing (epistemology) is hidden in science, and why the ways of knowing from the rest of the world is labelled as folklore, myths, religions, and culture, and traditions. Heavily influenced by Mignolo (1999, 2002, 2007) we have decided to engage in epistemic disobedience and de-link health and wellbeing from the magic of the idea of modernity and capital marketplace. In this, we are not completely rejecting what is useful from the Euro-North American sciences, however, point out that in a decolonisation process of knowledge we all—regardless of our histories, geographies, and contexts—have cultures, sciences, wisdoms, and knowledge. We are trying take our eyes away from the fantasy of the universality of knowledge and clear up a space where we might inject some ancient ideas to improve health and wellbeing of the contemporary and future human population and this planet, we call home (De Guzman et al., 2023).

Considering the climate crisis, disasters, conflicts, and uneven development challenges, in the contemporary world, transformation of health and wellbeing by reintroducing nature must be implemented within three different levels. What we propose here is not revolutionary as an idea. Many scholars from Asia, Africa, Latin/South America, and West Asia as well as many indigenous communities in North America, Australia, and New Zealand have pushed for these. However, we hope that the implementation of this idea might revolutionise health and wellbeing, which we are elaborating in the next chapter.

The first level of transformation must come from decolonisation of the mind. Over the past 500-years or more, we have learned European knowledge as universal. In that, we have lost or forgotten non-European knowledge that have been successful prior to the colonial project. The second level is that we must examine health and wellbeing beyond the capital marketplace. Health and wellbeing should be a value rather than a commodity. In that, everyone must have access to their basic needs, including food and nutrition, clean water and sanitation hygiene, and other necessities. Third level of this transformational process must be that health and wellbeing is everyone's responsibility. Combining with the first and second levels, the dominance of biomedicine, pharmacology, and businesses must be removed from the discourse of health and wellbeing.

While there are well trained doctors, improved technologies, and cutting-edge research, we are experiencing a downfall in health and wellbeing globally. In that, knowledge has become a problem rather than a solution, as it should be. In colonial mindset, commercial takeover of knowledge production, and manipulation of facts for profit are all related to knowledge. It was only in 2016, it was revealed that in the 1960s, the sugar companies funded Harvard University scientists to shift the blame from sugar to fat as being responsible for heart diseases (Kearns et al., 2016). Similarly, the pharmaceutical industry control not only research, but training of medical practitioners within the capital marketplace. Combining the industry control over research, medical journals are publishing articles without access to the actual clinical trial data, that medical practitioners then rely on to diagnose and treat their patients (Abramson, 2022).

In this, what we propose in the next chapter can become a useful framework in bringing collaboration between all knowledge systems and ways of knowing to facilitate improved health and wellbeing for everyone.

Sabbe Satta Bhavantu Sukhitatta
May all living beings be well.
A universal wish based on Buddhist spirituality and philosophy.

References

Abramson, J. (2022). *Big pharma is hijacking the information doctors need most.* TIME, April 28, 2022. https://time.com/6171999/big-pharma-clinical-data-doctors/. Retrieved on November 06, 2023.

Balon, R. (2006). Mood, anxiety, and physical illness: Body and mind, or mind and body? *Depression and Anxiety, 23*(6), 377–387.

Buddharakkhita, A. (1989). *Mettā: The philosophy and practice of universal love.* Buddhist Publication Society.

Butzer, K. W. (2012). Collapse, environment, and society. *Proceedings of the National Academy of Sciences, 2012*(109), 3632–3639.

De Guzman, K., Stone, G., Yang, A. R., Schaffer, K. E., Lo, S., Kojok, R., Kirkpatrick, C. R., Del Pozo, A. G., Le, T. T., DePledge, L., Frost, E. L., & Kayser, G. L. (2023). Drinking water and the implications for gender equity and empowerment: A systematic review of qualitative and quantitative evidence. *International Journal of Hygiene and Environmental Health, 247,* 114044. https://doi.org/10.1016/j.ijheh.2022.114044

Feola, G. (2015). Societal transformation in response to global environmental change: A review of emerging concepts. *Ambio, 44*(5), 376–390.

Firth, W. J. (1991). Chaos--predicting the unpredictable. *BMJ: British Medical Journal, 303*(6817), 1565.

Folke, C., Carpenter, S., Walker, B., Scheffer, M., Chapin, T., & Rockström, J. (2010). Resilience thinking: Integrating resilience, adaptability and transformability. *Ecology and Society, 15*(20).

Friedman, K. S. (2003). *Myths of the free market*. Algora Publishing.

Garro, L. C. (1990). Continuity and change: The interpretation of illness in an Anishinaabe (Ojibway) community. *Culture, Medicine and Psychiatry, 14*(4), 417–454.

Gidron, Y., & Ronson, A. (2008). Psychosocial factors, biological mediators, and cancer prognosis: A new look at an old story. *Current Opinion in Oncology, 20*(4), 386–392.

Gilgun, J. F. (2002). Completing the circle: American Indian medicine wheels and the promotion of resilience of children and youth in care. *Journal of Human Behavior in the Social Environment, 6*(2), 65–84.

Godbole, A., Sweta, & Abhinav. (2016). An Ayurvedic concept for prevention is better than cure. *World Journal of Pharmacy and Pharmaceutical Sciences, 5*(8), 414–420.

Graham, C., & Thomas, L. (2002). Using reasons for living to connect to American Indian healing traditions. *Journal of Sociology and Social Welfare, 29*, 55.

Hegde, B. M. (2019). *What doctors don't get to study in medical school* (4th ed., 553pp). Paras Medical Publishers. ISBN-10: 8181914198

Hegde, B. M. (2021). *உள்ளங்கையில் உடல் நலம்* (1st ed., 174pp). Sixth Sense Publications. ISBN: 9789387369207

Hele, K. S. (2020) *Anishinaabe*. The Canadian Encyclopedia, published online 16 July. Available at: https://www.thecanadianencyclopedia.ca/en/article/anishinaabe

Henning, D. H. (2002). *A manual for Buddhism and deep ecology* (Special). The World Buddhist University.

Hodge, D. R., Limb, G. E., & Cross, T. L. (2009). Moving from colonization toward balance and harmony: A Native American perspective on wellness. *Social Work, 54*(3), 211–219.

Jayawickrama, J. S. (2010). *Rethinking mental health and wellbeing interventions in disaster and conflict affected communities: Case studies from Sri Lanka*. University of Northumbria at Newcastle (United Kingdom).

Jayawickrama, J. S. (2023). "Those who make an enemy of the earth make an enemy of themselves": Climate change and human activities from a South and Southeast Asian perspective. In D. Madhanagopal, S. Momtaz (Eds.), *Climate change and risk in South and Southeast Asia: Sociopolitical perspectives* (pp. 19–35). Routledge.

Jhawar, S. R. (2004). *Building a noble world*. Noble World Foundation.

Kearns, C. E., Schmidt, L. A., & Glantz, S. A. (2016). Sugar industry and coronary heart disease research: A historical analysis of internal industry documents. *JAMA Internal Medicine, 176*(11), 1680–1685.

Krantz, D. S., Sheps, D. S., Carney, R. M., & Natelson, B. H. (2000). Effects of mental stress in patients with coronary artery disease: Evidence and clinical implications. *JAMA, 283*(14), 1800–1802.

Kudlu, C. (2016). Keeping the doctor in the loop: Ayurvedic pharmaceuticals in Kerala. *Anthropology & Medicine, 23*(3), 275–294.

Kuhn, T. S. (1962). Historical structure of scientific discovery: To the historian discovery is seldom a unit event attributable to some particular man, time, and place. *Science, 136*(3518), 760–764.

Kumar, H., Sharma, R. K., & Sharma, D. C. (2020). Understanding the relation between Mansik Bhavas and Vyadhi Utpatti W.S.R immunity. *International Ayurvedic Medical Journal*, 4461–4465.

Kutumbiah, P. (1962). *Ancient Indian medicine*. Orient Longman.

Lowery, C. T. (1998). American Indian perspectives on addiction and recovery. *Health & Social Work, 23*, 127–135.

Markley, O. M., & Harman, W. (1982). *Changing images of man*. Pergamon Press.

Max-Neef, M. A. (1991). *Human scale development: Conception, application and further reflections*. The Apex Press.

Mbiti, J. S. (1991). *African religions and philosophy*. Heinemann Publishers.

References

Mignolo, W. D. (1999). I am where I think: Epistemology and the colonial difference. *Journal of Latin American Cultural Studies, 8*(2), 235–245.

Mignolo, W. D. (2002). Geopolitics of knowledge and the colonial difference. *South Atlantic Quarterly, 103*(1), 57–96.

Mignolo, W. D. (2007). Delinking: The rhetoric of modernity, the logic of coloniality and the grammar of de-coloniality. *Cultural Studies, 21*(2–3), 449–514.

Mignolo, W. D. (2009). Epistemic disobedience, independent thought and decolonial freedom. *Theory, Culture & Society, 26*(7–8), 159–181.

Miñarro, S., Reyes-García, V., Aswani, S., Selim, S., Barrington-Leigh, C. P., & Galbraith, E. D. (2021). Happy without money: Minimally monetized societies can exhibit high subjective well-being. *PLoS ONE, 16*(1), e0244569.

Newman, M. A. (2000). *Health as expanding consciousness.* Jones & Bartlett Learning.

Newman, M. A. (2007). *Transforming presence: The difference that nursing makes.* FA Davis.

O'Keefe, P. (2020). Production of nature re-visited. *Antipode.* Online. https://antipodeonline.org/wp-content/uploads/2020/07/OKeefe-2020_Production-of-Nature-Re-Visited_Antipode-Online.pdf. Retrieved on January 03, 2023.

Pillay, A. (2019). *A critical review of the mainstream approaches to humanitarian aid practice and support systems: An autoethnographic inquiry into the social, political, and cultural experiences of a humanitarian aid worker.* PhD thesis. University of York, Health Sciences.

Prasad, V., Lenzer, J., & Newman, D. H. (2016). Why cancer screening has never been shown to "save lives"—and what we can do about it. *BMJ: British Medical Journal, 352.*

Prashad, V. (2014). *The poorer nations: A possible history of the global south.* Verso Books.

Prüss-Üstün, A., Bos, R., Gore, F., & Bartram, J. (2008). *Safer water, better health: Costs, benefits and sustainability of interventions to protect and promote health.* World Health Organization.

Radhakrishnan, S. (1950). *The Dhammapada: With introductory essays, pali text, English translation and notes.* Oxford University Press.

Radhakrishnan, S. (1963). *Bhagavad Gita.* George Allen and Unwin Ltd.

Rainey, L. D., (2010), *Confucius & Confucianism: The essentials.* Wiley- Blackwell.

Ray, O. (2004). How the mind hurts and heals the body. *American Psychologist, 59*(1), 29.

Ryser, R. C. (1997). Observations on 'Self' and 'Knowing', In H. Wautischer (Ed.), *Tribal epistemology: Essays in the philosophy of anthropology.* Routledge.

Sianipar, G. J. (2008). Poverty and global capitalism. *Studies in Philosophy and Theology, 8*, 91–105.

Sinclair, N. J. (2013). *Nindoodemag Bagijiganan A history of Anishinaabeg narrative.* The University of British Columbia.

Singh, B., & Gopal, R. K. (2016). Demystifying the brand patanjali—A case on growth strategies of Patanjali Ayurved Ltd. *PES Business Review, 11*(1), 51–66.

Smith, N., & O'Keefe, P. (1980). Geography, Marx, and the concept of nature. *Antipode, 12*(2), 30–39.

Stewart-Brown, S., & Farmer, A. (1997). Screening could seriously damage your health: Decisions to screen must take account of the social and psychological costs. *BMJ: British Medical Journal, 314*(7080), 533.

Sullivan, D., & Hickel, J. (2023). Capitalism and extreme poverty: A global analysis of real wages, human height, and mortality since the long 16th century. *World Development, 161*, 106026.

Tutu, D. (2004). *God has a dream: A vision of hope for our time.* Rider.

Watkinson, P., Barber, V. S., & Young, J. D. (2006). Strict glucose control in the critically ill. *BMJ: British Medical Journal, 332*(7546), 865–866.

Weaver, H. N. (2004). The elements of cultural competence: Applications with Native American clients. *Journal of Ethnic and Cultural Diversity in Social Work, 13*(1), 19–35.

West, B. J. (2006). *Where medicine went wrong: Rediscovering the path to complexity* (Vol. 11). World Scientific.

West, B. J. (2012). *Fractal physiology and chaos in medicine* (Vol. 16). World Scientific.

WHO. (2022). *World health statistics 2022: Monitoring health for the SDGs, sustainable development goals.* World Health Organization.

WHO. (2023). Malnutrition: Fact sheet. Available at: https://www.who.int/news-room/fact-sheets/detail/malnutrition/. Retrieved on December 22, 2023.

Wignaraja, P. (1991). *Participatory development: Learning from South Asia.* United Nations University Press.

Wolf, D. B., & Abell, N. (2003). Examining the effects of meditation techniques on psychosocial functioning. *Research on Social Work Practice, 13*(1), 27–42.

Wright, J., & Jayawickrama, J. S. (2021). "We need other human beings in order to be human": Examining the indigenous philosophy of Umunthu and strengthening mental health interventions. *Culture, Medicine, and Psychiatry, 45,* 613–628. https://doi.org/10.1007/s11013-020-09692-4

Zelinsky, W. (1975). The Demigod's dilemma. *Annals of the Association of American Geographers, 65*(2), 123–142.

Zhihua, Y. (2012). Taoist philosophy on environmental protection (pp. 279–292). In Z. Mou (Ed.), *Taoism.* Brill.

Chapter 5
Personal and Professional Encounters of Health and Wellbeing: Beyond Medical Sphere

5.1 Introduction

It is always challenging to divide between personal and professional encounters of health and wellbeing. While our encounters are personal, our professional encounters are also somewhat personal. The personal encounters of the two authors of this book are highly varied. The first author, Janaka, is a scholar with more than three decades of experience in international research, education, and humanitarian affairs. Much of his encounters with health and wellbeing are related to his childhood experiences, and his professional encounters that are during his collaborations with disaster, conflict, and uneven development-affected communities in Asia, Africa, the UK, and West Asia. The second author, Devendraraj is in the transition of early to mid-career researcher, and he is also a faculty member in a Jesuit Private University. Much of his professional experiences are based in Mumbai and Odisha, whereas much of his personal experiences are based in Tamil Nadu. This chapter begins with the experiences of the first author, followed by the experiences of the second author, and ends with a reflection and insights into the health and wellbeing.

5.2 Personal Experiences of Health and Wellbeing

Janaka's experiences on health and wellbeing started very early on. During 1974–1978, his family[1] lived in Hingurakgoda, then a small town in the North Central Province in Sri Lanka. At that time, the place was suffering from dire poverty; mostly seasonal farmers used to reside in this region. He grew up with friends who suffered from Malaria, malnutrition, and many other health issues. Absolute poverty lines are defined based on chosen basic needs, and relative poverty lines are based

---

[1] Throughout the section of this chapter, the third-person tense is used to refer to the first author, Janaka Jayawickrama.

© The Author(s), under exclusive license to Springer Nature Singapore Pte Ltd. 2025
J. Jayawickrama and D. Madhanagopal, *Reintroducing Nature into Health and Wellbeing*, https://doi.org/10.1007/978-981-96-3090-5_5

on the overall living standards of the community. Relative inequality of incomes in Sri Lanka declined between 1963–73 and deteriorated after 1973. The changes are broad-based; inequality of size distribution of personal family [spending units] and per capita income of Sri Lankans declined between 1963–73 and increased between 1973–82. The percentage of absolute poverty in the economy and within three major socioeconomic regions [urban, rural, and estate] declined significantly between 1963 and 73. Between 1973–79 and 79–82, the opposite occurred. The incidence of absolute poverty increased with such increases, most pronounced between 1973 and 79 (Divisekera, 1988).

The first experience that Janaka remembers was when a little friend of his died as he ate Dichlorodiphenyltrichloroethane—an insecticide used in agriculture (DDT) by thinking that it was sugar. As they lived in a tiny hut, the father of Janaka's friend did not have a safe place to keep insecticide and fertilizers. DDT used to come in boxes, and it is a white powder. Hence, no wonder a 3-year-old child thought it was sugar. Everyone in the region felt deeply sad. Although Janaka did not register this in how he understands life now, he felt life is unpredictable. The second experience—although not direct—was in 1979, when a cyclone severely hit the region that his family resided. This cyclone affected the lives of more than one million, took a toll of around thousand; it severely and partially damaged almost 250,000 houses of the residents, and it destroyed 90% of the coconut plantation of the Batticaloa district. It resulted in the government having to spend over Rs. 600 million to bring immediate relief to those affected (ADRC, 2003). He learned from his family and friends that huge numbers of cattle were killed in the cyclone and that hundreds and thousands of poor people sought protection by hiding under their beds or tables.

These two incidents have significantly impacted his thoughts about health and wellbeing, and his career choice. Importantly, he was a sick child who suffered from chest colds and contracted malaria twice, as well as other illnesses such as chickenpox and measles. As a result, he spent considerable time in rural medical facilities and urban hospitals receiving treatment. During this period, he observed that several rural healthcare workers, including doctors, were kind and committed, yet overloaded with multiple tasks, and they were largely exhausted. These were his early experiences with the Sri Lankan rural healthcare system in 1970s and early 1980s. In early 2000s, he got many opportunities to travel around the countries of the Global South as researcher and advocacy worker and learned that things have not changed much in between these decades.

Between 1979 and 1980, Janaka's family lived in Dambadeniya, a small town in the northwestern province of Sri Lanka. As a kid, Janaka continued to suffer from chest colds; his parents took him to a traditional medical practitioner—Wanamandawa P. J. Somaratne for treatment. The medical centre was located in Giriulla Puskoladeniya in Dambadeniya.[2] He vividly remembers his first meeting with Dr Somaratne. He talked for a long time with Janaka's parents and asked about their medical histories before talking to Janaka. Dr Somaratne wanted to know where Janaka slept, what he ate, when he would usually bathe, and almost everything about

---

[2] https://wanamandawe.lk/.

5.2 Personal Experiences of Health and Wellbeing

his daily routine, and he treated him with herbal remedies based on that. Also, he prescribed a three-month treatment plan with various herbal remedies. It was a painful and challenging experience. However, after three months, Janaka was fine and never had chest colds!

In 1981, Janaka's family lived in the Colombo district, where Janaka grew up without many health problems. Interestingly, Janaka's mother started using many home remedies to deal with common colds, stomach aches, etc. His mother began to develop terrible knee pain, and she could not walk, stand, or sleep. So, Janaka's family went to many different medical practitioners—from Western medical doctors to traditional medical practitioners. This went on for many months without a solution. In one instance, they went to a Buddhist Monk who was a traditional Sri Lankan medical practitioner (Deshiya Chikitsa).[3] The Buddhist Monk who treated Janaka's mother first diagnosed her condition as something to do with her memory, which had nothing to do with her brain. She was getting better gradually, and then they moved to Dambadeniya again. The year 1983 is an important year for all the Sri Lankan people. This was the year that the official war between the Sri Lankan Government and the Liberation Tigers of Tamil Eelam (LTTE) started.[4,5] Other than a three-month holiday from school, Sri Lankans did not experience the brutality of the events in July 1983. However, the events severely affected his relatives and friends (including Tamil friends), who lived in Colombo. 1983 marked the 30-year-old civil war in Sri Lanka, which killed many young men and women of both Tamils and Sinhalese. It also took away the lives of a Sri Lankan president and an Indian prime minister, among others.

During this period, Janaka's father started developing early signs of diabetes and high blood pressure. The Western medical doctor advised him to eat healthy rice or bread with vegetables and meat or fish. Also, he was instructed to do regular exercises and take Metformin, which at that time in Sri Lanka was a new medication. However, his diabetic condition did not get better, and his father developed angina. So, he was on more medication. For a short period, his father consulted with a traditional Ayurvedic practitioner in the Nittambuwa area, and the practitioner suggested him cut down on rice and bread entirely and increase the intake of vegetables; he introduced my father to fasting. This process happened in consultation with the Western medical doctor (as he was a family friend and did not like what his father was doing with the Ayurvedic medical practitioner). However, through this process, his father's diabetes started to go away. He felt much more agile, felt fit again, and lost weight.

However, later, a Western medical doctor finally won, and Janaka's father stopped this traditional treatment. He was back in Metformin and many other tablets. For the next 35 years, his father was on Western medication, of course, with increased dosages and more tablets each time. At the age of 80, his father was taking about 16 tablets daily and suffering through various discomforts due to side effects. Personally, this

---

[3] https://ayudeptncp.lk/en/featured/deshiyachikithsa/.

[4] https://humanityhouse.org/en/rampen-conflicten-sri-lanka-burgeroorlog-1983-2009/.

[5] https://www.sciencespo.fr/mass-violence-war-massacre-resistance/en/document/massacres-sri-lanka-during-black-july-riots-1983.html.

was a confusing experience for Janaka. What was working for his father with the traditional Ayurvedic practitioner was not accepted by the Western medical doctor. It was substantially successful in progressing the health conditions of his father, yet his father was told that it was unscientific and unhealthy in the long term.

5.2.1 Disasters and Crises: Health and Wellbeing

In 1997, Janaka met Dr Alison Eyre, a Canadian family physician who was living in Sri Lanka with her family. She came as an advisor to the organization that Janaka was working with, and they were providing assistance to displaced populations in Sri Lanka, especially in North and East at that time. Although, Janaka did not speak much English, and did not have a deeper understanding of issues related to health and wellbeing of displaced populations in Sri Lanka, Alison was kind towards Janaka and collaborated with him until the year 2000. In collaboration with Alison, Janaka started to explore the ideas on care, which later he realized is more important than medicine or medical interventions.

In 2000, Janaka studied and collaborated with the International Trauma Treatment Programme in Washington State of the United States of America. Dr John Van Eenwyk has been visiting Sri Lanka since 1997, and he became one of Janaka's mentors and changed Janaka's trajectory from being a humanitarian worker to an academic. That gave him the space and opportunity to understand the healthcare systems of the USA, which is claimed to be one of the most powerful and scientifically advanced nations in the world. In the Emergency Department of a hospital in Olympia, Janaka met with many people who suffered from toothaches, eczema, asthma, high blood pressure, and high cholesterol. Initially, he was shocked to learn that thousands of people in this "developed" nation were ignorant of preventing common and lifestyle-related ailments, and they are mainly dependent on Western biomedicine for every physical ailment. Above all, health and wellbeing are in the marketplace where people cannot access services without health insurance. Self-care and focusing on preventing diseases are some of the most neglected aspects of the lives of Americans. Then, after talking to doctors and nurses in the hospital, Janaka learned that they are waiting for simple health-related ailments to become emergencies so that they can receive free healthcare through emergency departments. Janaka also felt that there was nothing free in the USA, and almost every facility (including basic necessities) had become materialized and commoditized—so was health and wellbeing. Without health insurance, no one will be treated in any hospital, and the medical procedures in the USA are highly complex. It lies far away from the impoverished people Janaka met with many patients who had chronic alcoholism and drug addictions. They were trying to escape the harsh realities of life through these addictions. Although alcoholism and drug addiction in Asia are not less, he learned that many he met in the hospital and society, in general, were suffering from addiction in one way or another. Importantly, Janaka realized that Western biomedicine, practised in the USA, had lost touch with Western philosophies, which emanated

5.2 Personal Experiences of Health and Wellbeing

and evolved. Western biomedicine in North America and Europe has largely been systematically privatized, and it is only so helpful to the poor and the marginalized if there is direct support from the state. Along with this, he witnessed and experienced racism, discrimination, and the positive and negative sides of the USA during this period.

On December 26, 2004, the Asian tsunami happened. Before the tsunami, Janaka assisted a group working on environmental and sustainability issues in Sri Lanka to develop a disaster management project, the Disaster Management and Information Programme (DMIP). Through this Programme, Janaka and his team provided technical assistance in designing and developing the Disaster Management Act of Sri Lanka. On Sunday, December 26, when Janaka was at home, around 10.30 in the morning, a colleague from DMIP called him and said that the ocean was coming into the land. She asked him what they should do. Although Janaka studied disaster management, he had no idea how to respond to such emergency-related situations. However, he went in, and after about 2 h of the tsunami, he coordinated a national response; he effectively utilized all that he learned through his education and professional experience and implemented in this process. Overall, 13 coastal districts were affected in Sri Lanka, and his initial suggestion to the team was to conduct a damage assessment. As Janaka's team had a network of individuals and organizations nationwide, they successfully mobilized about 3000 volunteers to gather information about the adverse effects of the tsunami. He and his team worked tirelessly till the last day of December 2004. After giving a big effort, they successfully completed the first ever damage assessment report of the tsunami in Sri Lanka.[6] Janaka reflects on the impacts of the Tsunami and the ways in which he and his team collaboratively responded to the massive disaster and the vast threats that it brought to the millions of Sri Lankans in terms of health and wellbeing. Without any question, it was one of the most challenging and complex situations that he ever faced. Through the disaster response process, Janaka directly witnessed that both Sri Lankan traditional medicine and Ayurvedic medicine were immediately available and accessible to the disaster victims to deal with their health problems, and it significantly helped both people and the state deal with this massive challenge. Since millions of Sri Lankans were forced to be displaced, it naturally brought new challenges to them. Traditional medical systems of Sri Lanka were the ones that immediately helped them, but not Western biomedicine.

However, as Janaka identified that the international community response to the Tsunami in Sri Lanka was different, and not in par with the ground reality. They failed to recognize that in Sri Lanka, only 13 districts out of the total 25 districts were affected. Hence, half of the country was still able and functioning. Despite the tragic situation, Sri Lanka had a functioning governance system, and the state could somehow address people's health and wellbeing. Regardless of all these, the international responses created chaos and divided the country again through funding mechanisms. Janaka recalls that the 2004 Asian tsunami was the first time the global

---

[6] http://icsfarchives.net/8026/

humanitarian system received more than it requested in funding. As there was large-scale financial support from the international humanitarian agencies, there was no visible problem in accomplishing their allotted tasks. Sri Lanka received mental health experts from the USA who believed "hugging" would potentially reduce the "trauma" of disaster-hit victims. Many foreigners wanted to try out their practices and hypotheses on affected people.

> One morning a team of 'psychosocial specialists' came to our camp. We were told that they are from the US and here to help us to provide psychosocial activities. All of us gathered in the community hall and through translation they told us the importance of sharing our sadness and grief about our losses from the tsunami. Then the man and the woman who came from the US started hugging us. I felt very uncomfortable and irritated. During the tea break I went home and told my mother, and she told me to keep away from them.

(Jayawickrama, 2008, p. 4)

There are many similar stories like the above. However, the final evaluation of the Tsunami Evaluation Coalition (Telford et al., 2006) concluded the following, which is similar to Janaka's observations and experiences:

1. The international humanitarian community needs a fundamental reorientation from supplying aid to supporting and facilitating communities' own relief and recovery priorities.
2. All actors should strive to increase their disaster response capacities and to improve the linkages and coherence between themselves and other actors in the international disaster response systems, including those from the disaster-hit nations themselves.
3. The international relief system should establish an accreditation and certification system to distinguish agencies that work to a professional standard in a particular sector.
4. All actors need to make the current funding system impartial, and more efficient, flexible, transparent, and better aligned with principles of good donorship.

5.3 Encounters with Ayurveda: Insights from India's Southern Region

The second author of this book, Devendraraj's[7] experiences with health and wellbeing were different. He spent most of his young life in Tiruppur, a city in the western part of the state of Tamil Nadu in India—this city is popularly known as India's textile capital and knitted garments and is also known for pollution and migrant workers. Tamil Nadu is also one of the economically robust states India and became highly industrialized after 1980s (Kalaiyarasan, 2020; Muraleedharan et al., 2009). Also, Tamil Nadu is one of a very few states that possess robust public healthcare systems and internationally known for its achievements in health (Bango & Ghosh, 2023; Kumbhar,

---

[7] Throughout the section of this chapter, the third-person tense is used to refer to the second author, Devendraraj Madhanagopal.

2023). From his experience in Tamil Nadu, though Ayurveda and Siddha hospitals are substantially available and are accessible in many cities of Tamil Nadu, the population rely primarily on Western biomedicine. Given the increasing numbers of public and private hospitals (Western biomedicine) and the state's continued support towards it, it is naturally understood why people rely more on Western medicine. Besides that, the state, media, and the people primarily perceive biomedicine as one with more scientific backing than alternatives and more accessible than others. Since his childhood, he never tried neither Siddha nor Ayurveda for any of health-related illnesses, and as well as other local medicines. Looking back his childhood and adolescent periods, he remembers that there was no major epidemic hit Tamil Nadu other than Chikungunya and Dengue outbreak in the mid of 2000s and 2010s (Seyler et al., 2012; Chandran & Azeez, 2015). In the 2010s, whenever such disease outbreaks occurred, he often encountered health outbreaks associated with climate change in most media outlets. This trend became immensely common in the mid-2010s—as this period was also when South India, including Tamil Nadu and Kerala, became extremely hit by cyclones, floods, and heavy rains.

Whenever disease outbreak (particularly vector-borne diseases such as dengue and malaria) occurs in Tamil Nadu, particularly after 2015, it is often associated with changing climate, pollution, and hygiene issues in most media outlets and scientific articles (Chandy et al., 2013; Kakarla et al., 2019; Mutheneni et al., 2017; Imranullah, 2017), and the second author has witnessed the changing narrative and perceptions of people about diseases. However, everyday discussions on health and wellbeing in most media outlets in Tamil Nadu, and maybe in India as a whole, confine with hygiene, pollution, temperature, changing climate, and any other local and regional factors (Narayan, 2018), but it never extended into questioning Western biomedicine as whole. This is not to say that media outlets, state, and the public questioned medical systems. There have been several incidences of critiques against privatization of medical systems and inordinate expenditures and accessibility of private healthcare by the people and it was often highlighted in multiple forums. This has become high after COVID-19 (Jain, 2017; Newsclick, 2020; Raj, 2021). The second author has witnessed an unquestioned belief about the working and operating nature of Western biomedicine among the people in Tamil Nadu. However, people are largely aware of the side effects of drugs used in biomedicine, thanks to Television, print, and other social media outlets. Nevertheless, in this context, we must accept that there is widespread trust in biomedicine and its associated surgical techniques for almost all educated upper- and middle-class families in India. Over the past few decades, given the immense state support for public and private healthcare systems (Western biomedicine), this trend has already extended to the lower-middle and lower classes of Indian society, and they are mostly dependent on public healthcare systems at large.

Devendraraj's childhood and adolescent experiences with doctors were varied—not due to his sickness, but due to his mother's prolonged illness. She suffered from a rare form of muscular dystrophy, though none of her family members were affected by this illness, and there were no known genetic reasons. She developed this condition only in the middle of her 20 s, and it persisted until her passing away at around

48. Since it was a prolonged illness, Devendraraj's family consulted multiple doctors in nearby districts for her condition. This included not only Western biomedicine but also Ayurveda doctors. On various occasions, all the Allopathic doctors explained the difficulty of treating this rare illness, noting that it could not be cured completely. Still, they advised to prescribe various medicines continuously to her to keep the illness stable and not deteriorate further. Devendraraj's mother continued to take almost five tablets a day for years, and it provided multiple side effects for her. Despite this, and to not lose hope, they sought advice from various doctors for around ten years. Devendraraj's family also consulted Ayurvedic doctors at Arya Vaidya Sala Kottakkal, one of the prominent Ayurvedic hospitals in South India, for her treatment. She underwent some tablet-oriented Ayurveda medicine as well. Among all the medical encounters, Devendraraj's mother experienced some improvement in her condition for the first time, and she could perceive certain positive developments. Retrospectively, Devendraraj could recall the differences in the approach of Allopathic doctors and Ayurveda doctors from his adolescence experiences only to a limited extent. Allopathic doctors' approach towards patients has always been professional, formal, and limited. He witnessed multiple times that they suggested drugs to the patients without properly inquiring about the medical history and allergic backgrounds of the patients. The same happened with Devendraraj's mother.

Essentially, all the Allopathic doctors treat everyone in almost similar ways. For example, they neither engaged in personal conversations nor showed interest in knowing the medical history and background of the patients. More or less, they prescribe similar medicines to all the patients unless they find any sharp distinctions in the patient's symptoms. However, in the case of Devendraraj's mother, it was different. All the Allopathic doctors that she met with inquired about her family history curiously and wanted to know whether any of her family members were affected by similar kinds of illnesses; when they got to know there were none, they felt a bit disappointed and hesitatingly responded that there is no such complete remedy for this illness. His mother was naturally disappointed and anxious. After dabbling with various doctors and various forms of medicinal systems, Devendraraj's family ended up with Ayurveda, which worked relatively well, compared to other Allopathic doctors' prescriptions. However, she could not continue that due to her circumstances. We also point out Menon and Spudich (2010) interviews with cancer patients treated by Ashtavaidyas, a scholarly Ayurvedic physician in Kerala. Those patients shared similar experiences with Ayurveda—they noted that they felt better as it alleviated the side effects of chemotherapy and radiation therapy. The Ashtavaidyas could be able to manage the disease not to deteriorate further.

Having seen all these encounters with different medicinal systems and doctors/physicians as an adolescent boy, one thing that was common among all the medicinal systems (including Ayurveda) was that it increasingly became marketized and professionalized. Over the past two decades, with the adoption of neoliberal policies in India, increasing privatization in medical care and pharma, and underfunding of public healthcare systems have intensified the same (Borooah, 2022; Hooda, 2020). Hooda (2020) shows that in India, since the 1970s, state-led hospitals, hospital beds, and medical institutions have been declining, although the numbers vary nationwide. Importantly, underfunding of public healthcare systems and the current model of financing healthcare through an insurance-based mode, which is actually funded from public sources, have not been successful in delivering the health needs of millions and millions of poor and middle-class people of the country. This model of promoting the private sector through insurance is something new that has vigorously been pushed forward by India's union and state governments, particularly over the past two decades. Devendraraj vividly remembers that almost every time his family met with the doctor for his mother's treatment, they paid from their own pockets, which increased the financial burden on his father. There was no predominance of insurance availability in those days as in the contemporary period. Even today, claiming money from insurance for such prolonged illnesses remains a challenging task.

Devendraraj's experience with Ayurveda was much different than Janaka's experience, which shows that the experiences with traditional medical systems are not different to the experiences of modern biomedicine. He and his family consulted with Ayurveda physicians, who were like Allopathic doctors. His family did not understand the distinctions between the medicinal systems. In this context, it is essential to note the eroding knowledge base of Ayurveda physicians over the decades. On the one hand, classical and traditional Ayurvedic physicians have always been sceptical of increasing privatization of the medical profession and increasing trends of profit-making strategies in pharma and drug markets (both Western biomedicine and Ayurveda).

5.4 Towards a Conclusion

Both authors of this book spent considerable years conducting research in South Asia, including Sri Lanka and India. In particular, the first author possesses decades of international research experience in Sudan, Malawi, Jordan, Syria, Lebanon, Northern Iraq, Pakistan, Nepal, Kenya, and many other places during 2005–2019 on health and wellbeing. He spent some years on writing his PhD as well as spending time with a traditional Chinese medical practitioner in Newcastle upon Tyne in the UK. All our experiences collectively pointed us to the following conclusions. In many ways, it shapes our understanding of humanity. The external interventions in health and wellbeing might maintain a greater levels, their insensitivity continue to bring more uncertainties and dangers. The traditional systems maintain a low-level of health and wellbeing, however, this is sustainable.

In conclusion, we agree that sharing our selected personal experiences and encounters with Ayurveda and other traditional medical systems only provide a part of the understanding, and it will not capture the complexity, and breadth spanning traditional medical systems. Over the past few decades, mainly, liberalization has been strongly promoted in India and Sri Lanka by the respective states, leading to the commercialization of almost all traditional medical systems, and they are no longer practised in similar ways as they used to be a century ago. There are substantial noted exemptions in Ayurveda, Siddha, and Unani as some families continue to practise traditional medical systems and treat patients through herbs, alchemy, Yoga, and other indigenous systems of medicine for generations. For example, Ayurveda underwent various transformational phases over the past one hundred and fifty years or so—in both pre-and post-colonial India. Notably, the globalization of Ayurveda has happened over the past few decades—on the one side, it provides opportunities for Ayurveda to contact and engage with the outside world, and it also offers immense opportunities to increase the market values of Ayurveda and to protect the medical contributions of Ayurveda through intellectual property in the light of globalization. It spreads Ayurveda to the urban upper and middle class and foreigners. On the other side, it resulted in heavy systematization and formalization of herbal medicines Ayurveda—both education and practice, which was not the case centuries ago. Also, the herbal medicines of Ayurveda must pass through several quality control checkups of the foreign countries, and this has been a complex issue of concern by the manufacturers of Ayurveda medicine. Along with this many countries in the world are still not recognized as medicine as equally as Western medicine, and it has spread in the Western world as "quasi-medical healing" and "spiritual healing technique," which is problematic (Banerjee, 2004; Kasezawa, 2005).

In post-colonial India and Sri Lanka, Ayurveda went into transformation significantly and currently, we have two types of Ayurveda physicians. First, Vaidya (village or lineage-type practitioners) who are mostly not college-educated physicians and they learned through their lineage and family.[8] The second type is college-educated physicians (Kasezawa, 2005). In the case of the first author Janaka's family, they met with the former, who are Vaidyas, and those Vaidyas gave importance to the cultural logic to treat Janaka and his family members and they also did not separate mind from the body unlike the Western biomedicine usually does (Leslie, 1976; Nichter, 1981). In the case of the second author, Devendraraj's family was significantly different because the Ayurveda physicians that his family met with did not fall into both types. Though those physicians come from the traditional Vaidya family, they had formal education and continued to practise Ayurveda on par with Western biomedicine standards rather than the traditional way of treating the patients. Retrospectively, the second author realized that the treatment approach for his mother was more of a Western biomedicine. Jayasundar (2010, 2017) details the fundamental differences between Western medicine and Ayurveda in understanding the functions of human body through tridoshas (vata, pitta, and kapha)—this not only deals with physiological but also psychological functions of the body.

Overall, from our personal and professional experience, we find that people who rely on Ayurveda, Siddha, or Deshiya Chikitsa often for long-term illnesses and

---

[8] In recent decades, Vaidyas have increasingly sent their children to formal Ayurveda colleges. These college-educated Ayurveda physicians return to their family profession (Vaidyas) after completing their education. Overall, traditional Vaidya families have realized the importance of formal education in continuing to practise Ayurveda as societies become more modernized. They understand the necessity of adapting to societal norms and trends. The same applies to traditional Siddha Vaidya families as well.

5.4 Towards a Conclusion

complex conditions/illnesses that are difficult to treat with Western medicine. Time and again, research on traditional medical systems in both India and Sri Lanka shows that in recent decades, urban upper- and middle-class patients turn to Ayurveda, Siddha, and Deshiya Chikitsa, after Western medicine has failed them. After trying various Allopathic doctors and medical systems, they seek traditional medicine, which works well for some cases but not for many others. Over the past two decades, notable articles were published on the potentials and possibilities of Ayurveda to treat cancer and its side effects (Balachandran & Govindarajan, 2005; Sumantran & Tillu, 2012; Metri et al., 2013). However, not much has been discussed on how traditional medicine can be effectively treated or complemented with Western biomedicine for lifestyle-related complications and reduction of tobacco usage. Some of the recent works on these themes include (Semwal et al., 2015; Rathi & Rathi, 2020). Recently, in India, both Ayurveda and Siddha physicians and practitioners came forward to work with the Allopathy community to respond to the COVID-19 pandemic, and it worked to some extent in some regions of the country; however, in the long run, it did not go well as both the mainstream medical community and the state did not encourage it. Once vaccines for COVID-19 came, the roles of Ayurveda and Siddha practitioners suddenly declined and ended over the period.

Though Ayurveda, Siddha, and Deshiya Chikitsa are deeply interlinked with various philosophical schools of Hindu and Buddhist philosophies and their spiritual practices, in recent decades, both traditional medical systems practitioners have not treated their patients strictly along the lines of old norms—likewise, the medicines of Ayurveda, Siddha, and Deshiya Chikitsa. Traditional medical systems are highly standardized, formalized, and marketized today. Most importantly, the philosophical and spiritual insights that are the undercurrents of these medical systems are visibly missing. The nature and natural processes are increasingly lacking in traditional medical systems. For example, in Ayurveda and Deshiya Chikitsa, garlic is considered a powerful nerve stimulant and good for issues related to heart and cholesterol. However, in the past 25 years, many companies have been making garlic tablets for the market. What is missing in the tablets is the nature. The moment garlic gets processed, its nature changes, and it may not have the same natural qualities as its original form.

We can learn from ancient philosophies, historical experiences, and traditional medicinal systems that there is a need for a battle of ideas. The point of a battle of ideas is that it can facilitate clarity of thought, which develops theory. In return, there must be confidence among intellectuals to practise theory in society. The catch-22 here is that without clarity, one cannot practise, and without practice, one cannot maintain clarity. The point argued is that we need to learn from ancient and modern philosophies to shift the paradigm from attempting to produce nature to establishing a harmonious relationship with nature. This is a struggle that needs to be established. Stated again, the battle of ideas is where we find clarity and confidence to struggle.

References

ADRC. (2003). *Country report: Sri Lanka*. Available at: https://www.adrc.asia/countryreport/LKA/2003/index.pdf. Retrieved on July 28, 2023.

Balachandran, P., & Govindarajan, R. (2005). Cancer—An ayurvedic perspective. *Pharmacological Research, 51*(1), 19–30.

Banerjee, M. (2004). Local knowledge for world market: Globalising Ayurveda. *Economic and Political Weekly, 39*(1), 89–93.

Bango, M., & Ghosh, S. (2023). Reducing infant and child mortality: Assessing the social inclusiveness of child health care policies and programmes in three states of India. *BMC Public Health, 23*(1), 1149.

Borooah, V. K. (2022). Issues in the provision of health care in India: An overview. *Arthaniti: Journal of Economic Theory and Practice, 21*(1), 43–64.

Chandran, R., & Azeez, P. A. (2015). *Outbreak of dengue in Tamil Nadu* (pp. 171–176). Current Science.

Chandy, S., Ramanathan, K., Manoharan, A., Mathai, D., & Baruah, K. (2013). Assessing effect of climate on the incidence of dengue in Tamil Nadu. *Indian Journal of Medical Microbiology, 31*(3), 283–286.

Divisekera, M. S. D. K. (1988). *Income distribution, inequality and poverty in Sri Lanka, 1963–82*. Doctoral dissertation, University of Tasmania.

Hooda, S. K. (2020). Health system in transition in India: Journey from state provisioning to privatization. *World Review of Political Economy, 11*(4), 506–532.

Imranullah, M. S. (2017). 'Citizens" callous attitude to blame for spread of dengue. *The Hindu*, https://www.thehindu.com/news/national/tamil-nadu/citizens-callous-attitude-to-blame-for-spread-of-dengue/article20243021.ece. Retrieved on May 31, 2024.

Jain, Y. (2017). In 2017, India was caught between private exploitation and public sector callousness in healthcare. *The Wire*. 30 Dec. Available at: https://thewire.in/health/healthcare-aadhaar-national-health-policy. Retrieved on December 06, 2023.

Jayasundar, R. (2010). Ayurveda: A distinctive approach to health and disease. *Current Science, 98*(7), 908–914.

Jayasundar, R. (2017). If systems approach is the way forward, what can the ayurvedic theory of tridosha teach us? *Current Science, 112*(6), 1127–1133.

Jayawickrama. J. S. (2008). Ethical thinking: International mental health activities and communities. In D. Khoosal & D. Summerfield (Eds.), *Bulletin of Transcultural Special Interest Group (TSIG) of Royal College of Psychiatrists* (pp. 2–9).

Kakarla, S. G., Caminade, C., Mutheneni, S. R., Morse, A. P., Upadhyayula, S. M., Kadiri, M. R., & Kumaraswamy, S. (2019). Lag effect of climatic variables on dengue burden in India. *Epidemiology & Infection, 147*, e170.

Kalaiyarasan, A. (2020). Structural change in Tamil Nadu: Limits of sustainable development. *MIDS Working Paper No. 239*. Madras Institute of Development Studies.

Kasezawa, M. (2005). Ayurveda in the age of globalization: 'Traditional' medicine, intellectual property and the state. *Minamiajiakenkyu, 2004*(16), 85–110.

Kumbhar, K. (2023). The" Dravidian model": Egalitarianism and healthcare reform. *Indian Journal of Medical Ethics, 8*(1), 42–45.

Leslie, C. (1976). The ambiguities of medical revivalism in modern India. In C. Leslie (Ed.), *Asian medical systems: A comparative study* (pp. 356–367). University of California Press.

Menon, I., & Spudich, A. (2010). The Ashtavaidya physicians of Kerala: A tradition in transition. *Journal of Ayurveda and Integrative Medicine, 1*(4), 245.

Metri, K., Bhargav, H., Chowdhury, P., & Koka, P. S. (2013). Ayurveda for chemo-radiotherapy induced side effects in cancer patients. *Journal of Stem Cells, 8*(2), 115.

Muraleedharan, V. R., Dash, U., & Gilson, L. (2009). Tamil Nadu 1980s–2005: A success story in India. In *'Good health at low cost' 25 years on* (pp. 159–192).

References

Mutheneni, S. R., Morse, A. P., Caminade, C., & Upadhyayula, S. M. (2017). Dengue burden in India: Recent trends and importance of climatic parameters. *Emerging Microbes & Infections, 6*(1), 1–10.

Narayan, P. (2018). All mosquito-borne diseases on upswing in Tamil Nadu, malaria up 18%. *The Times of India*. https://timesofindia.indiatimes.com/city/chennai/all-mosquito-borne-diseases-on-upswing-in-tn-malaria-up-18/articleshow/62359388.cms?utm_source=contentofinterest&utm_medium=text&utm_campaign=cppst. Retrieved on May 31, 2024.

Newsclick. (2020). COVID-19: 'Set up committee for monthly audit of treatment, billing by private hospitals'. https://www.newsclick.in/COVID-19-Committee-Monthly-Audit-Treatment-Billing-Private-Hospitals. Retrieved on January 02, 2024.

Nichter, M. (1981). Toward a cultural responsive rural healthcare delivery system in India. In G. R. Gupta (Ed.), *The social and cultural context of medicine in India* (pp. 223–236). Vikas Publishing House.

Raj, G. V. (2021). Private hospitals fleecing Covid patients. *Deccan Herald*, 20 April. https://www.deccanherald.com/india/karnataka/private-hospitals-fleecing-covid-patients-976261.html. Retrieved on January 02, 2024.

Rathi, R. B., & Rathi, B. J. (2020). Ayurveda perspectives toward prevention and management of nicotine and alcohol dependence: A review. *Journal of Indian System of Medicine, 8*(1), 14–20.

Semwal, D. K., Mishra, S. P., Chauhan, A., & Semwal, R. B. (2015). Adverse health effects of tobacco and role of Ayurveda in their reduction. *Journal of Medical Sciences, 15*(3), 139.

Seyler, T., Sakdapolrak, P., Prasad, S. S., & Dhanraj, R. (2012). International perspectives: A Chikungunya outbreak in the metropolis of Chennai, India, 2006. *Journal of Environmental Health, 74*(6), 8–13.

Sumantran, V. N., & Tillu, G. (2012). Cancer, inflammation, and insights from Ayurveda. *Evidence-based Complementary and Alternative Medicine: eCAM, 2012*.

Telford, J., Cosgrave, J., & Houghton, R. (2006). *Joint evaluation of the international response to the Indian Ocean tsunami, Synthesis Report (110)*. ALNAP.

Chapter 6
Towards a New Paradigm

6.1 Towards a New Paradigm?

This is a chaotic and crisis time at a planetary level, involving human beings and Mother Earth. This is a chaotic time, yet we do not understand what it is to be human. The existing mainstream science, especially biomedicine, is limited in explaining human nature and answering this question. On one side, the Global North, the centre of coloniality, capitalism, globalization, and associated oppression, continued to play enormous political and economic roles in dominating the majority regions of the world, which is the Global South, which continued to be disgraced and damaged. This is a space where people are victimized, and conflict is prevalent.

As we conclude this book, we highlight that discussions regarding health in the Global South at the governance level, notably in countries such as India and Sri Lanka, tend to be associated with Western biomedicine. Mainstream Western biomedicine and the governance systems often disregard the traditional medicinal systems and usually regard them as secondary, with widespread rejection of ancient philosophies associated with them. Though much has been discussed on the integration of traditional medical systems and Western biomedicine (Nisula, 2006; Patwardhan et al., 2015; Rao, 2015; Spudich & Menon, 2014), discussions are regarding the associations of ancient philosophies of South Asia and its influence towards health and wellbeing, and how it can complement to the existing discourses of health and wellbeing. This book is one such attempt to begin those discussions—through this, we underline the impact of colonization on the people of the Global South and their traditional medicinal systems and how colonization and the current marketplace continue to guide our understandings and discussions towards health and wellbeing. In the early portions of this book, along with discussions on ancient philosophies, we have also highlighted the ways in which the state's approach towards health and wellbeing has largely inclined towards the privatization of healthcare settings, resulting in health delivery inequities and an overemphasis on treatments rather than prevention of diseases, and ensuring the wellbeing of the masses.

In this context, as a whole, this book stresses the ways in which to establish a process for collaboration between different knowledge systems. We reiterate that this book does not argue that either traditional medical systems or ancient South Asian wisdoms are better than any other knowledge system in the world. Rather, through this book, we point out that, given the precarious chaos and crisis we face as human beings, we must learn from every available philosophy and knowledge system—in particular, the traditional knowledge systems of South Asia offer immense possibilities for re-examining the modern problems of health and wellbeing, which we highlight.

6.1.1 Addressing the Challenges of Coloniality and "Epistemology"

Francis Bacon (1561–1626), the influential English philosopher, made large scholarly contributions to the development of the scientific method and is widely recognized as one of the founders of modern sciences and empiricism. Across the world, the sixteenth and seventeenth centuries witnessed a momentum of rise in scientific exploration. A leading intellectual of this period, Bacon contributed to epistemology—the theory of knowledge; his approach was to acquire knowledge through observation, experimentation, and inductive reasoning. Interestingly, this scientific method solely depends on the five human sensors—seeing, hearing, smelling, touching, and tasting. Bacon advocated for scientific knowledge based on empirical evidence rather than tradition, intuition, or abstract reasoning. His approach further led to the rejection of teleology, including the six essences: Earth, fire, wind, water, quintessential positive, and the act of God. He emphasized the importance of data gathering through systematic observation and conducting experiments to test hypotheses. Nevertheless, he overlooked the limitation of the five senses of humans in this scientific method.

From an experiential point of view, it is evident that human senses are limited. The typical human eye can only perceive light at wavelengths between 390 and 750 nm; the range of frequencies the human ear can pick up is usually cited as 20–20,000 Hz. Tasting and smelling are subjective experiences. However, humans' understanding of touch, which is still the complex nature of the process, has been poor and is not fully understood. This is because touching involves detecting pressure, temperature, and discomfort. The functionality of the human sensory organs depends on age, health, and environmental context. Our sensory organs are limited in function levels and by the amount of information they can provide. This certainly limits our perception of the world. Other non-human species have a different viewpoint/standpoint of Earth based on their sensory organs. With these limited sensory organs, human civilization developed advanced technologies, all the necessary comforts for living, and even venture to the moon. Despite all these stupendous achievements, we argue that we still possess a limited understanding of how to maintain health and wellbeing.

We perceive that there is a political issue in epistemology—to which Bacon has contributed significantly. Through mainstream science and education that has been

6.1 Towards a New Paradigm?

promoted by colonialism and the resulting capital marketplace, the world has been subjected to believe that there is only one way of knowing. This is essentially the European (and North American) epistemology. As advocated by Bacon, the epistemology of the Global North is based on systematic observation, experimentation, and inductive reasoning as the foundation for acquiring knowledge about the natural world. This epistemology has become the mainstream way of knowing, and according to scholars such as Illich (1973), Zelinsky (1975), Smith and O'Keefe (1980), Mignolo (1999), and Smith (1999), this epistemology has become more detrimental than beneficial. This epistemology from the Global North has contributed to the colonial project and the creation and maintenance of the capital marketplace, which has destroyed the natural evolutionary processes of more than half of the world's social, cultural, economic, political, and environmental structures. Mainstream institutionalized education has become a primary tool in indoctrinating people into this epistemology of the Global North.

Illich (1971) made the argument that institutionalized education creates confusion among students about processes and substances. In this education, students learn only one way to know and tend to believe that one epistemology derives from Europe (and North America). Of course, in former colonies, the students were beaten up until they left their traditional and cultural belief systems. For example, Janaka's father, who was born into the British Colony of Ceylon, was subjected to corporal punishment for speaking in his native language of Sinhala. They were told repeatedly that the Sri Lankan ways of knowing are wrong because they are unscientific. They were taught that the European ways of knowing are correct because they are scientific. However, more information is remembered in this education process, and the results improve. Students are taught that growth is success. As argued by Illich (1971), the student is confusing teaching with learning, a certificate with competence, a higher grade with education, and fluency with the ability to remember something new. Their imagination is trained to accept service in place of value.

Scholars such as Bush and Saltarelli (2000) and Smith (2000) have critiqued mainstream education for its repetitive nature and merely imbibing information to the students as knowledge without critical examination. Smith (2000) asserts that contemporary universities have become another corporate organization; financial benefits decide what debates happen and what approach society should follow regarding health and wellbeing. In this debacle, the "graduates" of mainstream institutionalized education mistakenly accept medical interventions for healthcare, regulations for freedom, and corporate competition for productive work. Health, wellbeing, learning, independence, imagination, and creativity are described in the individual's contribution to organizations, and their productivity depends on the management of institutions such as hospitals and schools.

Provided this background, in this book, we have highlighted that many different epistemologies derive from Asia, Africa, Latin, and South America, and West Asia, as well as through native populations in North America, Australia, and New Zealand possess potential to address health and wellbeing complications. However, mainstream epistemology derived from the global north continues to disregard these epistemologies as unscientific and romantic. According to the United Nations Educational, Scientific, and Cultural Organization (UNESCO, 2021), the epistemologies beyond the Global North can be defined as: "... *understandings, skills and philosophies developed by societies with long histories of interaction with their natural surroundings. For rural and indigenous peoples, local knowledge informs decision-making about fundamental aspects of day-to-day life. This knowledge is integral to a cultural complex encompassing language, classification systems, resource use practices, social interactions, ritual, and spirituality.*" This definition shows that knowledge may differ from observation, experimentation, and inductive reasoning. Mainstream knowledge can sometimes answer the question "how," but it is highly incapable of answering "why." For example, a physician can explain how a heart patient died. However, when it comes to why they died, we get multiple versions of answers.

Isha Upanishad, a principal Upanishad in the Vedantic tradition of Hindu philosophy, points towards the knowledge acquired without critical examination.

Andham tamah pravishanti ye avidyam upasate

tato bhuya iv ate tamo ya u vidyayam rataah.

[Translation: Into a blind darkness they enter who follow after the Ignorance, they as if into a greater darkness who devote themselves to the Knowledge alone].

Aurobindo (2003, p. 08)

Pointing out this, we assert that when someone continues to be ignorant, they will fall into blind darkness. However, the second line points out that while the knowledge acquired through the five senses is helpful in day-to-day survival or for certain aspects of life, it leads to darkness when it becomes a belief as the ultimate truth. As argued by Zelinsky (1975), the "Church of Science" is replacing or at least attempting to replace the "Church of Religion." According to this Upanishad verse, contemporary society is filled with vast amounts of information in the form of knowledge, yet this does not facilitate the health and wellbeing of billions of marginalized sections, and this does not facilitate harmonious relationships between humans and nature, which further leads to deterioration of balance. The risk of sensory-based knowledge is that the individual feels they know everything, believes it is correct, and cannot accept other perspectives. The colonizers believed their knowledge was superior to the ancient wisdom in Asia, Africa, the Americas, Australia, and West Asia. This often manifests as I/we know more; yours/theirs is poorer knowledge. We assert that this acts as a barrier to the ability of the mind to evolve further, and people defend with their limited information, which leads to an unreasonable sense of restlessness, followed by aggression, violence, destruction, and domination of others and nature. All this has a heavy toll on humans' health and wellbeing, which we often sideline to discuss.

Overcoming this massive challenge requires a transformation of mainstream education. The mainstream linear scientific analysis must allow an equal space for nonlinear scientific analysis. This requires an understanding beyond dissecting observation, experimentation, and inductive reasoning. Scholars such as Kimmerer (2013) explain that living things of all types provide an important lesson about the interconnectedness of life. In Isavsya Upanishad, the invocation of peace calls for an understanding of this interconnectedness of everything:

Om Poornamadah Poornamidam
Poornaat Poornamudachyate,
Poornasya Poornamaadaaya
Poornamevaavashishyate.
Om Shantih Shantih Shantih
That is full, this is full.
From the full emanates the full.
On taking the full out of the full, the full still remains.
Saraswati (2013, p. 13)

It is crucial in this understanding that there is no reason to divide the world—human vs non-human, geographies, races, genders, and other divisions we have seen in contemporary society. The Buddhist teachings show that both types of knowledge are helpful. In concluding this book, we propose a complete transformation in knowledge ranking between the Global North and Global South, which necessitates decolonization of the mind. This should happen to reintroduce nature into health and wellbeing, and we need to approach traditional medical systems deeply embedded into ancient wisdom and philosophical traditions without predetermined and prejudiced bias. As individuals, we can obtain knowledge through linear analysis. Nevertheless, the quality and breadth of any knowledge system can only be enhanced through sharing, practicing, and discovering within an environment that encourages seeking or continuing learning. Integrating various ways of knowing can actualize learning as a complex phenomenon inherent in every human being.

6.2 Health and Wellbeing Beyond the Capital Marketplace

In the contemporary period and the future, societies continue to consume resources at an exorbitant rate—this is continued to be driven by material development, the propagation of self-interest, exploitation, and profit-seeking. Daily life's aggressive and competitive nature, encompassing multiple activities like travel, work, education, and relationships, has introduced escalating stressors into people's lives (Prashad, cited in Podur, 2022). This makes humans incapable of dealing with life itself and ultimately impacts humans, non-humans, and the natural world. The prevailing narrative within capitalistic models stresses us to work diligently to support the marketplace and to enhance profits further—this secures sustenance and accumulates enough for a comfortable consumer-driven retirement. We know there is rarely any acknowledgment of reaching a point of sufficiency in any public discourses, both in developed and developing worlds; instead, the emphasis is on insatiable greed and acquiring material possessions for a sophisticated way of life.

We witness that colonial ideologies continue sweeping the contemporary world. Taming rivers, breaking prairies, clearing forests, and claiming the Earth for the benefit of humans have become a common theme in many development projects over the years. These self-destructive and earth-ravaging approaches to life and living will not suffice for humans to survive. A paradigm shift in our perspectives on nature is needed. Smith and O'Keefe (1980) argued that production in the capital marketplace cannot continue without the production of nature and space. However, due to the conflicting and unconscious process of controlling nature, what they found as the production of nature finally leads to destruction.

Within this context, the discourse of health and wellbeing is located in the same capital marketplace, which produces nature that results in destruction rather than establishing a harmonious relationship with nature and natural processes. As we discussed in previous chapters, mental and physical problems in the global population have been increasing at an alarming level. Uncertainty and danger in life are to be human and facilitate human beings to find their purpose in their exceptional struggle with nature and natural processes and each other. This is a human struggle, and the rules, methods, and tools are provided to them by the culture in which they grew up. According to Tucker (1931), the word culture originated from the Latin word "colere," which is a basic form of the verb "cole," which means "to till" and "to cultivate." In this, we argue that anyone's culture is based on their connection to Earth or nature. The seasons, geography, animals, insects, livelihoods, clothing, language, and many other aspects of human living can be connected to culture in this way. Each culture is a collection of guidelines that help human beings come to terms with the uncertainty and danger of life and practise compassion towards other human beings who are experiencing the same. Culture also allows human beings to deal with the fragility of life by explaining the reasons.

Regarding pain, sickness, and death, cultures provide massive support for individuals and communities. Every culture provides various methods to deal with suffering, and Illich (1975) argued that culture is a specific formula for health and wellbeing. As we explained in Chap. 4, the Global North has science and knowledge, and the Global South has culture and wisdom. The problem then becomes, without culture, how people are dealing with suffering. The current discourse of health and wellbeing, dominated by linear biomedical science in the capital marketplace, rejects uncertainty and danger to life. Medical doctors, insurance agents, and security experts are busy selling "products" that allegedly eliminate sickness, end the struggle against death, and promote happiness. What has become an industry is the denial of suffering through uncertainty and danger. As discussed in Chap. 4 and above, mainstream education does not facilitate any capacities within students to manage their own lives—body and mind—healthy eating, cultivating positive emotions, and effective methods to deal with external life challenges. The UNESCO Institute for Statistics (2022) claims that the global number of students pursuing higher education has doubled in the last two decades. What does this mean from a health and wellbeing point of view? Suppose we are to look for statistics on suicide rates, violent incidents

6.2 Health and Wellbeing Beyond the Capital Marketplace

against each other, communicable diseases, and mental health issues. Can we easily argue that education has not improved health and wellbeing?

In the same way that institutionalized education replaces learning with qualifications, the medical and pharmaceutical industry replaces cultural competencies to deal with suffering with painkillers, antidepressants, and various forms of medication and procedures. Many of the medications that are prescribed to reduce headaches, menstrual pains, and various forms of suffering are addictive, come with many side effects, and sometimes death itself. Most selective serotonin reuptake inhibitor (SSRI) antidepressants come with some of the following warnings[1]:

- *Some young people and adolescents have thoughts about suicide when first taking antidepressant. Be attentive to your mood changes.*
- *Antidepressant could weaken judgement, thinking, or motor skills.*
- *Report any new or worsening symptoms to your doctor, such as: mood or behaviour changes, anxiety, panic attacks, trouble sleeping, or if you feel impulsive, irritable, agitated, hostile, aggressive, restless, hyperactive (mentally or physically), more depressed, or have thoughts about suicide or hurting yourself.*

We highlight that is a small but typical example of the broader problem. The same drug is designed to mitigate suffering and can elevate more suffering in some other possible ways. This new suffering induced by the interventions that were designed to reduce suffering from uncertainty and danger to life is not only uncontrollable. Still, it has created torturous lives for many people. As argued in Ayurveda, Deshiya Chikitsa, Siddha, and many South Asian medical approaches, health and wellbeing can only be maintained through continuous lifestyle adjustments and holistic balance in everyday lives. Illich (1975) argued that the medical and pharmaceutical industry has significantly threatened health and wellbeing.

> The consequences of this continuing modernist deconstruction of mortality have brought us to the current postmodern impasse in which dying patients are trapped between two evils: a runaway medical technology of ventilators, surgeries, and organ transplants that can keep bodies alive indefinitely and – as if this prospect were not frightening enough – an understandable but reckless public clamour for physician-assisted suicide as the only alternative to such ignominious physician-assisted suffering.
>
> Morris, 1998; as cited by Heath (2002, p. 907)

Modern medical care, expected to facilitate the health and wellbeing of billions of people, has become increasingly depersonalized. People are being pushed into the advertising and exploitations of biomedicine, and the pharmaceutical industry is becoming disempowered. They accept medical professionals' diagnoses and interventions while falling into more suffering and harm. Angell (2008) points out that the medical industry dominates medical research institutions, while some universities have established research centres and teaching programmes funded by pharmaceutical companies. There is a conflict of interest in these cases, but the patients must pay the costs. Further, in their research, Cunningham et al., (2008, p. 1788) unexpectedly

---

[1] For example, warnings for antidepressants drugs can be found in the following websites URLs https://www.drugs.com/citalopram.html and https://www.uofmhealth.org/health-library/d00217a1.

found that mortality is either unaffected or decreases during doctors' strikes and may indicate that doctors have little impact on mortality. From a perspective of care and compassion, we argue that nurses and other hospital staff may have a bigger impact on mortality.

The current health and wellbeing practices being followed and implemented by most nations today are in a more profound crisis, similar to other institutions in the capital marketplace. This can result from the development of compartmentalized professionalism supported and encouraged by the capital marketplace to increasingly provide "better" healthcare for populations that have lost control of their health and wellbeing. Here, people are considered as "patients" or "unhealthy," and they do not have any authority to declare themselves healthy because a medical professional must certify that. Against this backdrop, we argue that health and wellbeing discourse, policy, and practice must be outside the greed, arrogance, and exclusion of the capital marketplace. The Bhagavad Gita, Chap. 16, Verse 21, explains that greed is one of the three gates that humans would create self-destruction (Radhakrishnan, 1963, p. 340). The contemporary marketplace promotes material development, selfishness, exploitation, and profits. These influences make human beings incapable of dealing with health and wellbeing and harm themselves and nature. In Dhammapada (Radhakrishnan, 1950), the Buddha explains that self-indulgence or greediness is the worst among all illnesses, and attachment creates the greatest sorrow (verse 203, p. 126).

Although the current discourse on health and wellbeing points towards physical, mental, and social factors, there is no discussion about spiritual aspects. In this instance, we define spirituality beyond religious definitions. Although misleading with the inclusion of spirit in the word, we define spiritual as beyond the human physical boundaries. For example, understanding that human beings cannot exist without nature and natural processes is spiritual. If one is strongly connected with nature and natural processes, then one can establish spiritual elements in health and wellbeing. Vader (2006) argued that physical, mental, and social dimensions of health and wellbeing are interrelated, and spiritual health, which points towards the sense and purpose of existence, is potent and interacts with other dimensions of health and wellbeing. Hawks et al. (1995) point out that supporting each other in groups and community, meditation, and imagery are various components of spiritual health and wellbeing in facilitating a meaning and purpose in life and connectedness to a larger reality.

Many physicists have commented on spirituality within the boundaries of science. David Bohm (1980, p. 221) explained that:

> Ultimately, the entire universe (with all its particles, including those constituting human beings, their laboratories, observing instruments, etc.) has to be understood as a single undivided whole, in which analysis into separately and independently existent parts has no fundamental status.

Similarly, Stapp (1977, p. 202) pointed that *"the fundamental process of nature lies outside space–time but generates events that can be located in space–time."* Goswami (1993, p. 141) explains that *"the universe exists as formless potentia in myriad possible branches in the transcendent domain and becomes manifest only when observed by conscious beings."*

6.3 Towards a New Paradigm for Health and Wellbeing

As discussed throughout this book, the ancient wisdoms of South Asian medical systems point towards a vital point: health and wellbeing are everyone's responsibility. By giving this responsibility to biomedical science, scientists and medical doctors have created a crisis in health and wellbeing globally. The quick fixes of the healthcare industry—from painkillers to organ transplants—create short-term relief; however, they build up long-term crises in populations. At the same time, traditional healthcare practices in South Asia and many other regions encourage lifestyle changes that align with nature and natural processes. It may maintain a low level from an outside perspective but facilitates sustainable health and wellbeing among populations (see Fig. 6.1).

As we underlined early in this book, human life is unpredictable. In that, sustaining health and wellbeing is a constant challenge. Uncertainty and dangers, including catastrophic life experiences, affect any individual's physical, mental, social, and spiritual wellbeing. Understanding the fundamental functioning of body and mind about society and nature is integral to sustaining health and wellbeing. All living beings, including humans and animals, have natural rhythms that vibrate, oscillate, and pulsate (Korn, 2013). In today's world, over 80% of chronic diseases are cancers and

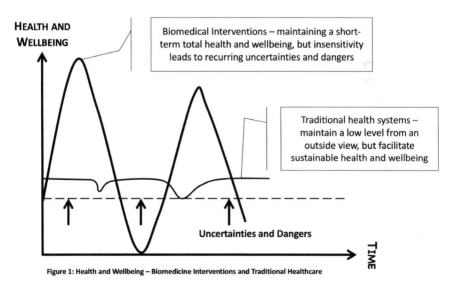

Fig. 6.1 Health and wellbeing—biomedicine interventions and traditional healthcare. *Source* Authors

heart-related diseases. We argue that only by understanding these chronic diseases within the natural context of the individual or populations is essential to approach the root causes of the problem. Obvious manifestations might prove to be a complex bundle of several interlinks that includes individuals, family, friends, community structures, the environment, and nature. We should not merely treat the symptoms of these diseases as it may delay the inevitable—it may further weaken the patient, and it may also lead to death. For most chronic diseases, healing the family and community could be essential in removing the numerous causes producing chronic conditions. Understanding the relationships between different and seemingly unrelated factors is essential for addressing the question of health and wellbeing (Ryser et al., 2017).

In this context, we propose this framework that can be used between individual medical practitioners and patients as well as in more extensive research processes. We argue that individuals and communities within their contexts possess a profound understanding of their environment and its natural processes, often surpassing the knowledge of medical practitioners and scientists, which are often essential in facilitating health and wellbeing. Those practicing wisdom possess insights into lifestyles, food habits, and other practices specific to their environment. This argument revolves around shared wisdom formed through experiential learning and communal sharing. The point is that addressing health and wellbeing within nature should begin with ancient wisdom and attempts to integrate modern knowledge systems. Here, it is important to note that traditional wisdom is not free from the influence of external factors. Various geopolitical and natural factors, such as colonialism, disasters, migration, wars, internal conflicts, and resource degradation, may have influenced, altered, or sometimes completely disrupted the traditional knowledge systems we possess today (Jayawickrama, 2010; Pillay, 2019). Collaborative partnerships between ancient wisdom and modern knowledge should be established, whether between individuals or larger groups, fostering mutual learning and equal participation. Such collaborations require compassion, care, and humility to build new knowledge (see Fig. 6.2).

The first step is collaboration among community members and external experts working towards the wellbeing of the community. This stage involves recovering the lost traditional knowledge systems over several generations. Importantly, this needs to be done by sensitive and reputed scholars, researchers, community elders, and other important individuals who ideally are recognized by the communities they work with, formally and informally. In this regard, through comparative data in a process involving examination and interpretation of experience on both the individual and group levels, elements may provide solutions towards sustainable conditions for addressing health and wellbeing and other issues such as human-nature conflicts. The effort in this regard should thus be collaborative; power dynamics will feature insiders in conjunction with outsiders (and external experts). This is then systematized (Jayawickrama, 2010; Pillay, 2019).

In the second phase, traditional knowledge recovery should be aimed systematically and validated within the specific context wherein it had occurred. After this, attempts can be made to share the recovered knowledge with the communities concerned—that should happen in an inclusive and participative process. Here, we

6.3 Towards a New Paradigm for Health and Wellbeing

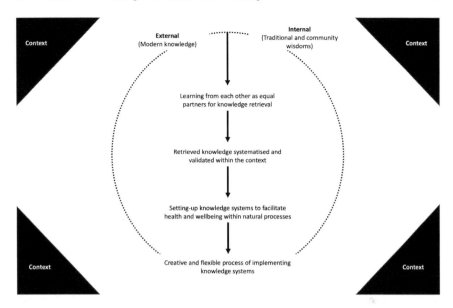

Fig. 6.2 Collaboration between modern knowledge and traditional wisdoms. *Source* Authors

need to ensure that sharing knowledge should occur in multiple forms—not just in the written forms in local languages but also through oral traditions, such as storytelling, theatre, poetry, and other more culturally relevant forms of expression that express human experience and creativity. Such retrieval, organization, and sharing processes should be seen as continuous. Here, we need to be open to receiving feedback from the people to reflect on their contexts, and we need to allow for an integrated evaluative process that can guide future actions. More importantly, many insights and lessons may emerge as part of such a process. The discourse must be removed from the analysis. The authentic partnership between external experts and community members will unlock the creative force of people to unleash their skills, leading to the third stage of this process. This creative force will further enhance the knowledge system; it fosters environmentally sustainable social, political, cultural, economic, and ecological interactions in individuals and communities. It will pave new pathways to enhance health and wellbeing harmonized with the natural process. It can create a new collaborative framework in which external and internal members will be treated as equal players/agents. Further development is encouraged in a way that does not alienate anyone. This process fundamentally differs from conventional scientific research or bureaucratic strategy, which typically treats communities as vulnerable objects and requires "external experts" to help them. Instead, our approach insists on a new "local" leadership form that collaborates with insiders and external experts. People take ownership of their health and wellbeing and leadership in promoting health and wellbeing within their families and communities. In other words, collaboration looks to better power sharing as a better balance between external and internal actors (Jayawickrama, 2010; Pillay, 2019).

The fourth and final step of this framework is social, cultural, economic, political, and environmental responsibility to challenge and transform previous practices to improve health and wellbeing. These transformations that we conceive should not be based on the usual top-down models; instead, great adaptability is required which considers the complexity and unpredictability of the system. We intend that it does not rely on fixed objectives that emerge from top–bottom—instead, it operates through self-correction, internal review, and continuous feedback. Mobilization, cooperation, and organization form a nonlinear process; it goes through setbacks and challenges. People will go through a process of action, reflection, and goal achievement, motivated by their values and holistic knowledge system, until the set objectives are attained. This empowers individuals and communities and enhances their capacity for health and wellbeing (Jayawickrama, 2010; Pillay, 2019).

This requires knowledge systems to be approached very differently from the conventional approach that is being followed in our academic institutions today. We identify three types of knowledge: (1) Knowing how—This to understand the process or method by which something can be achieved or done. (2) Knowing that—This refers to being certain that something is true or real, without needing further evidence. (3) Knowing if—This involves exploring whether something is true or not. Evidence-based understanding can give an account of how things work, even though the operationalization of "how" knowledge is not always required. For example, someone could quit drinking alcohol without giving any clear reason for the change. In contrast, becoming a yoga practitioner usually involves following specific steps and relying on clear evidence (Ryser et al., 2017).

The second type of knowledge is based on an intuitive understanding that something exists or not. According to Indian Philosopher Radhakrishnan (1937), this type of knowledge is knowing through intuition—this is direct, and mostly, it occurs without apparent evidence based on logic or experience. For example, a person can say instinctively by seeing the first glimpse of a butterfly—"This butterfly is great!"—it is intuitive knowing. This does not require facts, data, or rational argument but on a direct, emotional, or sensory experience. However, intuition typically comes up as a result of sudden awareness or insight spurred by stimuli either within or outside of a human. Another typical example is that a mother knows that her child is not feeling well, even if the test results provide no proof of any illness. In such a case, even an experienced paediatrician would depend on the instinctive feeling of the mother because it forms an intuitive perception related to her child, often beneath the level of consciousness (Ryser et al., 2017).

The third type of knowledge attempts to answers the question "if"—this emerges from deliberate, mindful action aimed towards an intended outcome. For instance, when a diabetic person decides to try his or her longest fast at the hope of reducing insulin levels, he/she may find that it really does work. This represents an emerging knowledge from testing one hypothesis and either confirms already known knowledge or opens up new knowledge.

In brief, experimentation or exploration is what "if" knowledge is all about. If the outcome works out as expected, it becomes a validated form of practical knowledge that will either reinforce an already existing knowledge or one that comes to be transformed (Ryser et al., 2017). What we explained throughout this book on health and wellbeing is somewhat against the linear scientific understanding of knowledge production. This is against mainstream epistemology based on the reductionist approach of observations and experiments. In most ancient traditions from Asia, Africa, Latin/South America, and West Asia, as well as among indigenous populations in North America, Australia, and New Zealand, many different epistemologies produce new knowledge. They have survived for centuries without modern scientific knowledge, and as explained in Chap. 4, some of them did very well until the European colonizers arrived on their shores. As we point out in Fig. 6.2, the possibility of collaboration between modern knowledge and ancient wisdoms, therefore, requires compassion, care, and humility.

We propose that compassion can be understood as a wish for others to be free from all sufferings and the causes of suffering. Compassion involves valuing everyone's mindsets, especially when we would not wish to endure the same ordeal. Similar to this, care involves the inclusion of an idea or another living being in one's life without any discrimination. In this collaboration framework, it is essential to establish care from this perspective so that there will be no discrimination of ideas, knowledge, or practices without giving equal opportunity to explain within the context. Finally, humility can be understood as the experience of the world and everything in this world, with wonder in the realization that everything is interconnected. Humility is essential in this framework to establish solid and equal collaborations.

References

Angell, M. (2008). Is academic medicine for sale? In K. D. Pimple (Ed.), *Research ethics*. Routledge.
Aurobindo, S. (2003). *Isha Upanishad: Translation and commentaries* (Vol. 17). Pondicherry: Sri Aurobindo Ashram Press.
Bohm, D. (1980). *Wholeness and the Implicate Order*, London: Routledge and Kegan Paul.
Bush, K. D., & Saltarelli, D. (2000). *The two faces of education in ethnic conflict: Towards a peacebuilding education for children*. United Nations Publications.
Cunningham, S. A., Mitchell, K., Narayan, K. V., & Yusuf, S. (2008). Doctors' strikes and mortality: A review. *Social Science & Medicine, 67*(11), 1784–1788.
Goswami, A. (1993). *The self-aware universe*. Putnam.
Heath, I. (2002). Endpiece: Trapped between two evils. *British Medical Journal, 324*, 907.
Hawks, S. R., Hull, M. L., Thalman, R. L., & Richins, P. M. (1995). Review of spiritual health: Definition, role, and intervention strategies in health promotion. *American Journal of Health Promotion, 9*(5), 371–378.
Illich, I. (1971). *Deschooling society*. Harper & Row.
Illich, I. (1973). *Tools of conviviality*. Harper & Row.
Illich, I. (1975). *Medical nemesis*. Calder and Bryers.
Jayawickrama, J. S. (2010). *Rethinking mental health and wellbeing interventions in disaster and conflict affected communities: Case studies from Sri Lanka, Sudan and Malawi*. University of Northumbria at Newcastle.
Kimmerer, R. (2013). *Braiding sweetgrass: Indigenous wisdom, scientific knowledge, and the teachings of plants*. Milkweed Editions.
Korn, L. E. (2013). *Rhythms of recovery: Trauma, nature, and the body*. Routledge.

Mignolo, W. D. (1999). I am where I think: Epistemology and the colonial difference. *Journal of Latin American Cultural Studies, 8*(2), 235–245.

Nisula, T. (2006). In the presence of biomedicine: Ayurveda, medical integration and health seeking in Mysore, South India. *Anthropology & Medicine, 13*(3), 207–224.

Patwardhan, B., Mutalik, G., & Tillu, G. (2015). *Integrative approaches for health: Biomedical research, Ayurveda and Yoga.* Academic Press.

Pillay, A. (2019). *A critical review of the mainstream approaches to humanitarian aid practice and support systems: An autoethnographic inquiry into the social, political, and cultural experiences of a humanitarian aid worker.* PhD thesis. University of York, Health Sciences.

Podur, J. (2022). Talking to Vijay Prashad about "Modernization". *Countercurrents.* Available at: https://countercurrents.org/2022/01/talking-to-vijay-prashad-about-modernization/. Retrieved on February 03, 2024.

Radhakrishnan, S. (1937). *An idealistic view of life.* Unwin.

Radhakrishnan, S. (1950). *The Dhammapada: With introductory essays, Pali text, English translation and notes.* Oxford University Press.

Radhakrishnan, S. (1963). *Bhagavad Gita.* George Allen and Unwin Ltd.

Rao, G. H. (2015). Integrative approach to health: Challenges and opportunities. *Journal of Ayurveda and Integrative Medicine, 6*(3), 215.

Ryser, R. C., Gilio-Whitaker, D., & Bruce, H. G. (2017). Fourth world theory and methods of inquiry. In P. Ngulube, (Ed.), *Handbook of research on theoretical perspectives on indigenous knowledge systems in developing countries* (pp. 50–84). IGI Global. https://doi.org/10.4018/978-1-5225-0833-5.ch003.

Saraswati, S. S. (2013). *Ishavasya Upanishad.* Yoga Publications Trust.

Smith, L. T. (1999). *Decolonizing methodologies: Research and indigenous peoples.* Zed Books.

Smith, N. (2000). Afterword: Who rules this sausage factory? *Antipode, 32*(3), 330–339.

Smith, N., & O'Keefe, P. (1980). Geography, Marx, and the concept of nature. *Antipode, 12*(2), 30–39.

Spudich, A., & Menon, I. (2014). On the integration of Ayurveda and biomedicine: Perspectives generated from interviews with Ashtavaidya Ayurveda physicians of Kerala. *Current Science*, 1500–1504.

Stapp, H. P. (1977). Are superluminal connections necessary? *Nuovo Cimento, 40B*, 191–204.

Tucker, T. G. (1931). *A concise etymological dictionary of Latin.* Ares Publishers.

United Nations Educational, Scientific, and Cultural Organisation. (2021). Local and Indigenous Knowledge Systems (LINKS). https://en.unesco.org/links. Retrieved on January 06, 2024.

United Nations Educational, Scientific, and Cultural Organisation. (2022). *Higher education figures at a glance.* UNESCO Institute for Statistic.

Vader, J. P. (2006). Spiritual health: The next frontier. *The European Journal of Public Health, 16*(5), 457–457.

Zelinsky, W. (1975). The Demigod's dilemma. *Annals of the Association of American Geographers, 65*(2), 123–142.

Index

A
Africa, 2, 9, 15, 18, 19, 32, 38, 51, 92, 97, 113, 114, 123
Ancient, 5, 7–14, 16–20, 25, 27, 28, 30, 38, 52, 57–59, 61–63, 65–67, 70, 71, 78–80, 84, 86, 89–91, 107, 111, 112, 114, 115, 119, 120, 123
Ayurveda, 11–14, 20, 28, 52, 54–60, 63–67, 69, 70, 77–81, 87, 88, 102–107, 117

B
Biomedical, 4, 13, 18–20, 34–40, 47, 52, 53, 56, 64, 65, 69, 79, 81, 83, 86–88, 116, 119
Biomedicine, 4, 13, 17, 18, 30, 32–35, 37, 39, 41, 46, 52, 55, 60, 70, 75–78, 80, 86, 93, 100, 103–107, 111, 117
Buddhist, 7, 11–14, 16, 17, 19, 28, 54–57, 59, 61, 65, 79, 81–83, 89, 90, 93, 99, 107, 115
Buddhist philosophy, 12, 13, 83

C
Capitalism, 3–5, 30, 46, 111
Capital marketplace, 3, 9, 14, 17, 18, 29–31, 38, 42, 46, 47, 64, 71, 80, 83–85, 89, 91–93, 113, 116, 118
Care, 29, 37, 38, 40, 46, 47, 64, 78, 80, 83, 87, 88, 100, 104, 117, 120, 123
Collaboration, 16, 80, 83, 86, 88, 93, 112, 123
Colonialism, 4, 7, 89, 113
Coloniality, 3–5, 66, 71, 111
Colonial project, 14, 18, 29, 31, 92, 113
Communities, 2, 5, 6, 9, 15, 16, 18, 32, 54, 71, 92, 97, 102, 116, 120
Compassion, 38, 70, 80, 83, 87, 88, 116, 118, 120, 123

D
Decoloniality, 4
Decolonisation, 4, 92
Deshiya Chikitsa, 11, 12, 14, 20, 46, 55, 56, 64, 77, 80, 81, 83, 87, 88, 99, 106, 107, 117
Development, 1–4, 8, 14, 16, 29, 32, 38, 40–42, 44, 58, 60, 66, 68, 70, 87, 89, 91, 92, 97, 112, 115, 116, 118
Disease and illness, 40
Dualism, 35, 43, 90

E
Education, 2, 3, 9, 14, 16, 17, 32, 36, 37, 41, 42, 62, 66, 69, 81–83, 85–87, 89, 97, 101, 106, 112–117
Environment, 2, 5, 7–9, 12–15, 28, 41, 42, 47, 65, 71, 77, 82, 88, 90, 115, 120
Epidemics, 5, 6, 33, 36, 43, 45, 52
Epistemic freedom, 17, 18
Epistemology, 4, 13, 17, 38, 66, 70, 71, 89, 92, 112–114, 123
Euro-North American, 12, 13, 17, 66, 86, 89–92
Europe, 3, 4, 9, 30, 32, 33, 37, 40, 44, 54, 56, 66, 91, 92, 101, 113
European Enlightenment, 4, 31, 47

© The Editor(s) (if applicable) and The Author(s), under exclusive license to Springer Nature Singapore Pte Ltd. 2025
J. Jayawickrama and D. Madhanagopal, *Reintroducing Nature into Health and Wellbeing*, https://doi.org/10.1007/978-981-96-3090-5

Index

G

Globalization, 3, 20, 37, 78, 106, 111

H

Health, 2–11, 13–20, 25, 27–29, 32, 33, 35–43, 45–47, 51–53, 56–60, 64–68, 70, 71, 75, 77–88, 90–93, 97–105, 111–120, 123

Health and wellbeing, 2, 3, 5, 6, 10, 13–20, 29, 41, 47, 51–53, 59, 65, 70, 71, 78–81, 84, 86–88, 90–93, 97, 100, 105, 111, 114, 116–120

Healthcare, 1, 19, 36, 37, 41, 46, 51, 55, 57, 79, 86, 98, 100, 102, 103, 105, 111, 113, 118, 119

Hindu, 7, 11–14, 16, 17, 19, 28, 38, 54–57, 61, 65, 67, 79, 89, 107, 114

Human, 1–7, 9, 11–13, 18, 19, 28, 30–32, 35, 36, 38, 41–43, 47, 51, 52, 57, 60, 61, 64, 65, 67, 70, 71, 75–80, 82–84, 88, 90, 91, 106, 111, 112, 115, 116, 118, 119

Humility, 80, 87, 88, 120, 123

I

Impermanence, 10

India, 2, 4, 7, 12–16, 18–20, 31, 45, 52, 53, 55–61, 64, 66–69, 77, 78, 86, 92, 102–107, 111

Indigenous, 6, 32, 52, 55, 56, 61, 66–68, 92, 106, 114, 123

Intervention, 37

K

Knowledge, 3, 4, 7, 9, 12, 13, 16, 17, 25, 29, 31–34, 37, 42, 52–54, 56–59, 61–63, 66–68, 70, 71, 75–77, 86–89, 91–93, 105, 112–116, 120, 123

M

Medical sciences, 1, 87

Modern, 5, 17, 19, 25, 27, 30, 31, 36, 38, 39, 41, 44, 68, 69, 71, 75, 77, 78, 89, 107, 112, 120, 123

Modernity, 3–5, 13, 30, 89, 92

Modern medicine, 36, 69

N

Nature, 2–9, 11–14, 17–20, 25, 28, 29, 32, 35, 38, 41, 42, 45–47, 52–55, 57, 61, 64, 65, 70, 71, 75–79, 84, 86–88, 90–92, 103, 107, 111–116, 118–120

North America, 3, 4, 9, 18, 32, 40, 41, 83, 92, 101, 113, 123

P

Philosophies, 5, 7–9, 11–14, 16–20, 29, 32, 46, 54, 56, 57, 70, 71, 80, 86, 89, 100, 107, 111, 114

Planet, 4, 7, 9, 18, 41, 42, 47, 71, 76, 78, 82, 90

Population, 39

Poverty, 1, 2, 14, 15, 17, 19, 43, 46, 51, 76, 84, 85, 97

Production of nature, 30, 42, 91, 116

S

Science and technology, 4, 33

Scientific analysis, 15, 19, 30, 47, 91, 114

Siddha, 11–14, 20, 28, 52, 54–57, 60–65, 69, 70, 77–80, 87, 88, 103, 106, 107, 117

South Asia, 2–4, 7, 9–17, 19, 51, 52, 54, 56, 57, 66, 69–71, 76, 78, 80, 82–84, 87–89, 92, 105, 111, 112, 119

Spirituality, 62, 84, 93, 114, 118

Sri Lanka, 2, 7, 12, 14–20, 39, 52, 55–57, 61, 64, 76, 81, 83, 86, 92, 97–101, 105–107, 111

Suffering, 1, 4, 9, 11, 19, 36, 75, 77, 78, 81, 84, 97, 99, 100, 116, 117, 123

T

Traditional medical systems, 5, 12, 17, 19, 20, 28, 52–54, 57, 66, 69–71, 84, 87, 105, 107, 111, 112, 115

Transformation, 6, 32, 33, 86–88, 92, 106, 114, 115

U

Uncertain, 11, 62

W

Wellbeing, 1–3, 5–9, 11, 13–20, 25, 29, 32, 36, 38, 41, 46, 47, 51–53, 56–58, 63–66, 70, 71, 75, 78–82, 84, 86–88, 91–93, 97, 98, 100–103, 105, 111–120, 123

Western biomedicine, 32–35, 75, 77, 78, 100, 103, 106

Wisdoms, 13, 31, 32, 54, 80, 89, 90, 92, 112, 119, 123

Printed in the United States
by Baker & Taylor Publisher Services